THE
THREE GUNSALLUS BROTHERS

FIGHTING FOR PENNSYLVANIA DURING THE CIVIL WAR

BY

Edward Leo Semler Jr.

Copyright © 2016 by Edward Leo Semler Jr.

All rights reserved by the author.

First Edition: 2016

Library of Congress Control Number: 2016903350

ISBN: 978-0-692-65318-0

Printed in the United States of America

Cover layout by Edward Leo Semler Jr.

To the descendants of the Gunsallus family.

TABLE OF CONTENTS

Introduction	1
Preface	7
1861	11
1862	17
1863	39
1864	61
1865	93
Post War	107
Resources	113
About The Author	117

INTRODUCTION

This book is the true story of three brothers, John, Samuel, and Taylor Gunsallus, who fought for the state of Pennsylvania during the American Civil War. Waged from 1861 to 1865 it consumed the lives of nearly a million Americans. The fighting was some of the most ferocious in American history and sadly pitted Americans against each other. As you read this book you may be stunned by the levels of death and destruction Americans wrought, witnessed, and endured during the war.

The brothers were the sons of Michael Meese Gunsallus and Ruth A. Lucas who had a total of eight children; John being the 1st child, Samuel the 4th, and Taylor the 5th. Raised on the family farm in Snow Shoe, Pennsylvania the brothers were well versed in handling a gun and riding a horse; skills that would prove to be valuable when they went off to war. And the Gunsallus' had a history of fighting for their country. They could trace their roots back to their great-great-grandfather, Richard Gunsallus (1756-1838), who fought with the Pennsylvania Militia from 1776 to 1778 in the American Revolutionary War.

Located just off of Interstate 80 in the rolling hills of Centre County, in central Pennsylvania, Snow Shoe is a small rural community. There are many Pennsylvania Amish in the area who live without electricity, and it is common to see them riding along the roads in their horse drawn buggies. So you get the feeling not much has changed from the mid 1800's when this story takes place. There are still many Gunsallus's and their extended family who live there. And fittingly there is even a Gunsallus Road.

Gunsallus Road in Snow Shoe, Pennsylvania

I was first introduced to my Civil War heritage, John Gunsallus is my great-great-grandfather, by my grandmother Grace Gunsallus Semler. John was her grandfather and had lived with her and her parents, Harry and Annie, on Gunsallus Road in

Snow Shoe until his death. Grace was 7 years old when he passed away.

I was very close to my grandmother and even lived with her during my senior year of High School in Allison Park, Pennsylvania. She had moved to McKees Rocks, Pennsylvania in her later years and while visiting her there in the late 1980's she told me she wanted to entrust me with a valuable document. I said I would be honored. Reaching under her bed she pulled out a large brown bag and handed it to me. Inside the bag was a large framed certificate. The frame seemed newer but the certificate was definitely old. It was written in black ornate cursive and the only color was a faded blue seal in the upper left corner. As I tried to read the elaborate cursive I could make out that it was a promotion certificate for a 1st Lieutenant John Gunsallus of G Company, 51st Regiment Infantry, Pennsylvania Volunteers, and dated the 13th of February 1865.

Not remembering my grandmother's maiden name I asked her who John Gunsallus was, and she said he was her grandfather. I then wrapped the certificate back up in its brown bag and assured her that it was in safe hands. Not having an immediate impact on me I took the certificate home and hung it on my wall. And although it was placed in a predominate location, it remained their pretty much unnoticed for almost 25 years.

Grace Gunsallus Semler

Every now and then the certificate caught my attention and I wondered what John Gunsallus experienced in the war. The internet wasn't around at the time and my motivation low, so researching John and the 51st really never "grew any legs" as they say. I lived off and on in Western Maryland and Pennsylvania, near numerous famous Civil War battlefields, and I would occasionally go visit them and see if they involved the 51st regiment. And that was about the extent of my research into John Gunsallus and the Civil War.

Whenever the topic of our Civil War ancestors came up with other family members there were all sorts of family legends. The most prominent was that Grace had 6 uncles who all fought at the Battle of Gettysburg and the only one who survived had gone home on leave to visit his sick mother. Although that story is pretty much false, you'll find as you read this book that there is some truth to parts of it.

It wasn't until my wife became interested in genealogy that the true story of John Gunsallus and his brothers started to unfold. After visiting Snow Shoe and the Askey Cemetery, where many of the Gunsallus family are buried, I became really interested in my great-great-grandfather and his involvement in the Civil War. Subsequent research revealed that his bothers Samuel and Taylor also fought for Pennsylvania. The more I researched, the more their stories revealed the history of my family and that of the United States of America.

And John's certificate which hung quietly on my wall took on a whole new significance to me as I learned more about him. What had once seemed like a simple recognition of achievement was now opening the door to a compelling story of three brothers.

PREFACE

This book could not have been compiled without the enormous amount of time and effort spent by those I give credit to in the reference section of this book. My three ancestors did not leave many documents to help me personalize or detail their time in the service, such as diaries or letters home - that I am aware of.

However I was able to obtain copies of John, Samuel, and Taylor's military records from the National Achieves which, along with other documentation, had a majority of their Company Muster Roll Cards. These cards identify on a monthly basis, among other things, which company and regiment they were attached to. And by following the company and regiment they were attached to, I can subsequently follow them. As an example; I have a Company Muster Roll Card showing John was attached to G Company of the 51st Regiment Infantry, Pennsylvania Volunteers during September 1862. It's a fact that the 51st fought at the Battle of Antietam in September 1862. So John was at the Battle of Antietam.

Something I found interesting with the documents in my research, which you may notice, was the many different ways the surname Gunsallus was spelled. John, Samuel, and Taylor did not fill most of these documents out themselves, they were completed by clerks who more than likely wrote the name as they thought it sounded. I'm also not sure how educated each brother was and if all three could read or write, so this may have added to the problem when they were asked to spell their names.

I was also able to locate photographs from the Library of Congress that depict some of the major milestones in this story. Photography was in its infancy during the 1860's so they are not the clearest, but they certainly provide a visual record of what the brothers actually saw.

Finally, books and articles that I read, researching this book, seemed to get into the weeds about what every regiment, division, corps, and general was doing at the same time as their subject. I realize that their intention was to give the reader a broad understanding of what was going on surrounding their subject, but I found this very confusing and distracting. Especially when you are following three men, each in a different regiment. So I tried to limit this broader view of the war and its leaders, and tried to instead keep the focus of the story on the Gunsallus brothers and their regiments.

| G | 51 | Pa. |

John Gunsallus

1" Sergt, Co. G, 51 Reg't Pennsylvania Inf.

Appears on

Company Muster Roll

for Jan & Feb, 1863.

Present or absent... Present

Stoppage, $............100 for...............

Due Gov't, $............100 for...............

Remarks: Appointed 1st Sergt.
Jan. 11/63. Vice
Campbell promoted

*Borne in present column
as John Gunsaulus.

Book mark:...............

Haxxel

(858)   Copyist.

Sample of a John's Company Muster Roll Card

1861

Tensions were high between the Union, and Confederate States entering 1861. And when Fort Sumter, South Carolina, a Union fort, was attacked by the Confederates on the 12th of April men clamored to enlist in their respective armies. And John Gunsallus was among the first wave to enlist on the 24th of April.

John was 23 years old, 5 feet 11 inches tall, of dark complexion, with grey eyes, and black hair. He was employed as a lumberman and lived with his parents in Snow Shoe, Pennsylvania. With a sense of duty and patriotism John travelled to the nearby town of Bellefonte and joined B Company of the 10th Regiment Infantry, Pennsylvania Volunteers. He enlisted as a private for a period of 3 months and would be paid $13.00 a month. The 10th was one of many regiments only enlisting men for a period of 3 months. I'm sure that's probably all the time the United and Confederate States thought it would take to march to the battlefield and resolve the issue between them.

The 10th regiment mustered-in at Camp Curtin at Harrisburg, Pennsylvania on the 26th of April. The camp was named in honor of the sitting Governor of Pennsylvania, Andrew Curtin.

Five days later John and the regiment loaded up on rail cars and were transported to Chambersburg, Pennsylvania. Here they encamped at Camp Slifer where they were provided with barracks, complete with new straw to sleep on. Although well housed the Army had not yet established its food logistics and there was nothing to feed the men. But the local townspeople stepped forward to save the day and kept John and the 10th well fed with all sorts of fresh baked goods, meats and produce.

While at Camp Slifer John and the 10th were issued their uniforms and equipment. They also began to conduct military drills which taught them how to march in formation. Army life for the most part was good at Camp Slifer. But with so many men living in close quarters, with only basic sanitary conditions, disease and sickness set in. And before they had a chance to fight John's B Company lost 2 men to illness, Privates Charles H. Winters and Samuel Armbister.

On the 8th of June John and the 10th left Camp Slifer and marched 11 miles to Greencastle, Pennsylvania where they encamped near Camp Meredith. Then on the 25th they marched another 21 miles to St. James College, Maryland. The men were not use to marching such long distances with all their equipment and were worn out. They would have plenty of time to catch their breath as they stayed there for the remainder of June. Their mission was to keep an eye out for Confederates operating in the area, but they never encountered any.

Then on the 1st of July the regiment was ordered to head south into Virginia. Excited to get into the action John and the 10th

crossed the Potomac River and headed toward Martinsburg, West Virginia. On the way they came across destroyed crops and property, the calling card of the Confederate Cavalry operating in the area.

On the morning of the 3rd of July John's B Company was sent forward of the regiment to help support a Union Cavalry regiment that was looking for the Confederate Cavalry. They encountered them near Berkeley, West Virginia killing 1 man and wounding 2. By afternoon John's Union contingent had liberated Martinsburg from Confederate hands to the relief of the townspeople.

Continuing to march 16 miles south toward Bunker Hill, West Virginia the 10th regiment along with a larger Union force began to encounter the remains of more and more abandoned Confederate campsites. The number of them alarmed the Union men as it indicated a larger Confederate force then theirs. Changing course they marched 12 miles east to Charles Town arriving on the 17th of July. Here John and the Union Army found little sympathy from the people of Charles Town as they were Confederate sympathizers.

Leaving Charles Town on the evening of the 20th John and the 10th joined up with Union Artillery and other infantry regiments to form a line of battle outside of the city. But no battle was fought here because the Confederates had fallen back to fight further south at the First Battle of Bull Run.

By the 23rd of July John and the 10th were nearing the end of their short 3 month enlistment. I guess the Union Army thought the war would not go on much longer and they sent John and the 10th regiment back home to be demobilized. Reaching Harrisburg on the 31st of July John and the rest of the men of the 10th regiment were paid and mustered-out of service. John returned to Bellefonte where he had enlisted and found work as a laborer.

The quick war that both sides thought would only last a few months was now dragging into its sixth month with no end in sight. And now both armies began to mobilize more men to the battlefields for the longer than expected war.

John once again enlisted on the 20th of September 1861, this time with G Company of the 51st Regiment Infantry, Pennsylvania Volunteers. On the 17th of October his new regiment again formed up at Camp Curtin in Harrisburg and he was officially mustered-in once more as a private, making $13.00 a month. He received his pay in cash every two months, or when the pay master was able to catch up with the regiment.

Mustering-in at Camp Curtin the 51st formed up all the various companies that had been recruited for the regiment. Companies A, C, D, F, and I were recruited in Montgomery County, E, H, and K in Union and Snyder Counties, G in Centre County, and B Company in Northampton County. So like most Civil War regiments on both sides of the fight, the men more than likely knew each other. And the men in these companies certainly knew each other and were related, friends and neighbors.

The time spent at Camp Curtin was consumed with being assigned uniforms, weapons and day upon day of drills, which continued throughout the war. Drilling was very important for a military regiment of the period. Battle engagements were conducted in a very formal and deadly way, with men marching toward each other out in the open. As they were shelled and fired upon they held formation until they were close enough to fire. This strategy proved very costly for both sides. But the time spent drilling before actual combat taught John and the men of the 51st the discipline to march into battle, fire, and proceed on.

In their free time they wrestled and tossed each other in the air via a blanket, which was a favorite. But once again, having so many men together in camp brought on health problems and several men died due to poor sanitary conditions. This was problematic throughout the war and amazingly most regiments lost just as many men to disease as to combat.

Before John and the 51st left Camp Curtin they were presented their colors (flags) by Governor Curtin who told them *"Return with them with honor, or return not at all."*[12]

On the 15th of November as snow gently fell, John and the 51st boarded a train for Annapolis, Maryland. Upon arrival in Annapolis three days later they were initially housed at Saint John's College, then moved to the old French burial grounds outside the city. On the 20th they moved again, this time about 2 miles outside of Annapolis and named their new home Camp Union. Time in Annapolis was spent drilling and providing guard duty for the city. John's Company did not do any fighting but lost Private William P. Hall to an illness.

1862

On the 6th of January, as part of a 15,000 man expeditionary force to North Carolina, John and the 51st boarded vessels at the Naval Academy in Annapolis. Companies A, C, F, and K embarked on the schooner *Scout* and companies B, D, E, G, H, and I embarked on the *S.S. Cossack*. In total about 80 ships finally set sail on the 9th and head out in to the Chesapeake Bay. Once out in the open waters of the Atlantic Ocean the group of vessels ran into a storm and the heavy seas slowed the flotilla to a crawl. The journey was taking longer than expected and as the days dragged on their provisions ran low. The men were now sea sick and had run out of drinking water. They were forced to drink vinegar and catch what rain water they could dripping from the sails of the vessels. I'm sure the cramped living conditions also added to the strain of being at sea. On John's schooner there was an outbreak of sickness in D Company and several of the men died.

Finally on the 5th of February after a month at sea the fleet anchored in Croatan Sound, North Carolina and awaited further orders. The next day the fleet was escorted by the *USS Philadelphia* to Roanoke Island, North Carolina. After Union Navy gunboats provided a heavy artillery barrage to soften the Confederate defenses they were finally put ashore on the 7th.

The Battle of Roanoke Island was underway. The following day the 51st engaged the enemy who were still dug in and heavily fortified, even after the artillery barrage. The 2,500 Confederates had established their defensive position in the middle a swamp. The only access to their fortification was by a single causeway which was covered by their artillery. Even though heavily fortified the Union force overran the Confederate outpost and captured it, taking quite a few prisoners. The 51st depicted their captured foe *as "uneducated wild men!"*

The Union lost 37 men with 214 wounded. The Confederates lost 23 men with 58 wounded and 62 missing. The 51st did not play a prominent role in the attack and John's company only sustained one wounded man, Private James Dolan.

As John and the regiment settled into their new quarters, supplied by the Confederates, they drilled and prepared for the next fight. The 51st stayed at Roanoke Island until the 3rd of March when they were embarked on vessels that took them to New Berne, North Carolina. The following is an interesting firsthand account of the event from a reporter, which puts into a nutshell how the military operation unfolded;

"We embarked (the 51st Pa. Vol.) on board the steamer 'Cossack' and schooner 'Scout' on the morning of the 3rd, and expected, from the orders received at the time, to arrive at our first destination long before now; but it seems the navy was not ready to co-operate with the land forces until yesterday, in consequence of their not being able to get their required supply

of ammunition, military stores, etc., in due season. Yesterday, at 2 p.m., we received orders to be in readiness to sail at 6 a.m. this morning, having been lying at anchor upon the quiet waters to Croatan Sound for eight days, and when the word came to get up steam the boys hailed it with great satisfaction. A life on the 'Ocean wave,' to a 'Land-bublet,' becomes dry and irksome after a few days. Give them terra firma and they are contented, but keep them aboard ship and they lose their wanted glow of spirits, energy and military discipline."[7]

Ten days later on the 13th of March they finally disembarked about 15 miles from New Berne and prepared for battle. The 12,000 men of the Union went up against 4,000 well-fortified Confederate troops. This time the 51st played a pivotal role helping to move artillery pieces into place. This was a monumental task because the roads were deep with mud from torrential downpours. *"You can imagine our situation, marching with heavy knapsack, three days rations in their haversacks, sixty rounds of ammunition and all the paraphernalia of a common solder, and then tugging away with these six howitzers and caissons full of shot and shell for fourteen miles, you can imagine what each soldier had to do, and often the wheels went down in the mud up to the axles."*[12] Exhausted the regiment made camp in a pine forest in the pouring rain.

The next day the two armies engaged each other on the 14th of March in a dense fog. After moving the artillery pieces again, to get them into position, the 51st moved ahead and held fast. The regiment was exhausted from the chore and appreciated the break to catch their breath. While resting they watched the first wave of their Union companions charge the Confederate stronghold but come up short when they exhausted their ammunition before taking the defenses. The 51st was then called up to continue the charge. Having to traverse a ravine filled with felled trees John and the regiment rushed past the first wave of their comrades, who had come up short with their charge. As they passed them they were cheered on in their rush to the fortification. Overtaking the enemy the regiment charged into the Confederate stronghold and Corporal George W. Foote of E Company planted the colors of the 51st on the fort. From here they advanced on the city of New Berne. Without a fight the Confederates fled the city destroying as much as they could before it fell into Union hands. By evening, with New Berne secured, John and the 51st made camp on the banks of the Neuse River *"without shelter in a drenching rain, and the air cold and chilling and the ground soaked with rain, with only a cup of coffee to go to sleep."*[12]

The Union was victorious but at a cost. The Union lost 90 men with 380 wounded and 1 missing. The Confederates lost 60 men with 100 wounded and 400 captured. The 51st had two men from D Company seriously wounded.

The following day a detail of men from the 51st was sent out to bury the Union and Confederate dead. In one rifle pit alone they came across the bodies of 14 Confederates. They were also sent to a nearby plantation to procure food, which happened to be owned by a Confederate Cavalry officer who was away fighting. They followed their orders and only took what was needed.

After the victory at New Berne the 51st was primarily used as a reconnaissance force deployed to the interior of Confederate held North Carolina. Two of the major missions were the Expedition to Pollocksville March 21st and 22nd, and the Expedition to Elizabeth City from April 16th to the 22nd. These two missions gathered valuable intelligence on the enemy and also helped secure important military objectives along the coast.

The Expedition to Pollocksville's objective was to burn three bridges. At 0700 on the 21st of March John and the regiment marched 24 miles to Pollocksville and burned all three bridges without resistance. With their mission accomplished the regiment returned to New Berne arriving late the next day.

On the 16th of April the 51st were loaded up into the steamer *Admiral*. They disembarked on the 19th about 4 miles from Elizabeth City in chest deep water and had to wade ashore. After drying out their clothes the 51st led a Union force of 3,000 men, which marched nearly 20 miles inland searching for the enemy. Without warning the two advance scout companies of the 51st, Companies A and F, engaged a heavily fortified Confederate post at Camden consisting of about 1800 defenders.

After heavy volleys of small arms fire from both sides the engagement subsided and the Confederate force drifted back into the countryside. As they fell back they destroyed several bridges in an attempt to slow the Union advance. But the Union force was too exhausted to pursue their foe. The heat and long march had taken its toll and they returned to their boats. It was a costly day for the 51st as they lost 3 men with 21 wounded. Two of the wounded were from John's Company; Privates Theophilus Baird and James Powers. Overall the Union lost 12 men with 98 wounded. The Confederates lost 6 men with 19 wounded.

On the 20th of April the Union force made it back to the landing where they had disembarked the previous day. Within 24 hours John and the Union force had marched 42 miles and fought a battle. As they waded out to embark upon the *Admiral* they were worn out. The 51st arrived back at New Berne with the rest of the Union force from the fight at Camden on the 22nd of April. They remained there drilling until the 2nd of July when they received orders to once again embark on vessels. To keep the mission a secret the regiment was issued sealed orders and told not to open them until out at sea. Companies E, H and K boarded the schooners *Thorn* and *Mystic* and John and the remaining companies boarded the schooner *Recruit*. As the vessels made their way out to sea the sealed orders were opened and their destination was revealed as Hampton Roads, Virginia. But before the regiment could get there the Union Army changed their battle plans and they were turned back and offloaded at New Berne.

On the 6th of July they once again boarded the schooner *Recruit* which took them to Fortress Monroe, Virginia. Arriving two days later they proceeded on to Newport News, Virginia arriving on the 9th of July. While there John and his companions drilled and spent their free time fishing, foraging, bathing, and playing baseball. And on the 27th as the Union Army was growing the 51st became part of the newly formed IX Corps.

On the 2nd of August the 51st boarded the schooner *Restless* and disembarked on the 4th of August at Aquia Creek, Virginia. From here they boarded rail cars of the Aquia Creek and Fredericksburg Railroad which took them to Fredericksburg, Virginia. Arriving on the 5th they made camp in a wheatfield near the station. There they found themselves with several other regiments heading to Fredericksburg as part of a larger Union force being put together for a major upcoming campaign.

Aquia Creek, Virginia showing transport vessels[16]

Back home in Centre County, Pennsylvania the newly formed 148th Regiment Infantry, Pennsylvania Volunteers was signing up men to fight the ever growing war. John's younger brother Samuel was one of the first to join. Following John's footsteps the 21 year old traveled from the family farm in Snow Shoe to nearby Bellefonte. He signed up on the 8th of August and was assigned to H Company as a private making $13.00 a month, like his brother John.

As the dead and wounded started to return home from the battlefields men were not as eager to join as they were at the start of the war. As an incentive men were now being offered bounties to sign up. Samuel took advantage of this and was awarded a sign up bounty of $100.00, which would be spread out in payments over his enlistment. The day he mustered-in he was given the first installment on his bounty which was $25, plus a $2 premium. And *"in the evening of the 8th day of August, 1862 in the public square in front of the court house these men were first formed in line. They were inspected and hurriedly examined by Dr. Fairlamb who pronounced them fit for service, they were then dismissed for the night."*[2]

The following day Samuel and his company were cheered as they loaded into wagons which took them to Lewistown, the closest railroad line, where they boarded rail cars bound for Harrisburg. During the transit the boxcar Samuel's company was travelling in caught fire. Troops were usually transported in boxcars with straw placed on the floor to sit on and someone smoking may have inadvertently caught the straw on fire. As the smoke became dense one man fearing for his life jumped from the moving train. Finally Corporal Alexander Gibb and Private Hiram H. Clapp volunteered to try and stop the train. They were swiftly lifted to the roof of the car and made a daring dash to notify the train's operator. The train was eventually stopped and the fire extinguished. The man who had jumped from the train was found dead where he had landed and was buried there by the side of the railroad tracks. Finally reaching Harrisburg on the 16th they joined the rest of the company's making up the 148th regiment and mustered-in at Camp Curtin.

Meanwhile John and the 51st were up and moving on the 12th of August and marching along the Rappahannock River. As they marched the weather was cold and as usual it was raining. The following day they were still on the march when they received the bad news that 4 members of the regiment had died. They were heading back home on convalescent leave aboard the vessel *West Point* and drowned when she sank on the Potomac River. One of the men who perished, Private James Gummo, was from John's Company.

On the 14th of August the regiment made it to Bealton Station, Virginia where they boarded rail cars of the Orange and Alexandria Railroad.

Late in the day they arrived at Culpepper Court House, Virginia and made camp. The following day John and the regiment marched 5 miles in the rain to Raccoon Ford, Virginia where they were tasked with repairing the road there.

Orange and Alexandria Railroad cars[6]

After completing their task John and the Union force continued to march, once 29 miles in eight hours. While marching they engaged the enemy in numerous skirmishes in Northern Virginia as they pushed along toward the Second Battle of Bull Run. The weather was rainy with torrential downpours. On the 23rd of August the lightning was so fierce it struck a caisson loaded with ammunition and blew it up. Although encountering the enemy on several occasions John's Company did not sustain any casualties.

As John and the 51st made their way across Bull Run Creek on the 29th they arrived on the battle field amid a roar of artillery as the two armies clashed. *"By this time the battle was raging in all of its fury, the air was simply filled with shrieking and exploding shells, and the dying and wounded were being carried to the rear by the hundreds."*[12]

The intense fighting lasted until dark. The regiment held its position as they supported an artillery battery who was shelling the enemy. The battle raged on through the following day until the Union force withdrew from the battlefield toward evening. Like at the First Battle of Bull Run the Confederates came away with a victory. As the Union withdrew, the 51st helped cover the rear and positioned itself on several occasions to protect the orderly withdrawal. Although being involved in several skirmishes during the battle and withdrawal, John's Company only sustained two casualties; Privates John Miller and William Moore who were wounded. The rest of the 51st sustained 4 wounded, 7 captured and 1 deserter. The Union Army did not fare as well losing 1,716 men with 8,215 wounded and 3,898 missing or captured. The Confederates lost 1,305 men with 7,048 wounded.

One of the more prominent Confederate generals during the war and at the Second Battle of Bull Run was General Thomas "Stonewall" Jackson. John and the 51st actually went up against his Corps at Second Bull Run. Many years later in the mid 1980's my family lived in Manassas, Virginia very close to the battlefields where the fighting occurred during both Bull Run engagements. General Jackson was so influential in both engagements that a High School was named in his honor in

Manassas, and my sister Ann graduated from it - Stonewall Jackson High School.

As the 51st moved back to the north they encountered the enemy on numerous occasions in light skirmishes without sustaining any casualties. Reaching Washington, DC on the 5th of September they made camp within sight of the Capital building. Leaving Washington two days later they continued to head north. Marching for several days they finally reached the outskirts of Frederick, Maryland on the 12th. The march was punctuated by more heavy rain. But the land was ripe with fruit and the men of the 51st picked what they could as they proceeded on.

Marching through Frederick on the 13th of September and Middletown, Maryland the following day the Union Army came upon the Confederates at the Battle of South Mountain;

"The artillery having cleared the mountain of the enemy, the 51st was soon ordered to advance towards the summit of the mountain, and on our march passed in one pile at least fifty dead rebels, and on reaching the top of the mountain witnessed the same thing, only there was at least one hundred and twenty-five dead rebels laying stretched acrossed each other along the stone wall, On the crest of the mountain ran a narrow lane protected by a stone fence on either side. The enemy had used the position as a sort of breastworks and all along this lane there was a sight to be seen. Along its whole length the rebels laid in piles up to the very top of the stone fence. Some were found in a kneeling position in the act of

firing. Death to many of them must have been instantaneous. Their arms extended and in position as in the act of firing, and in some cases the bitten cartridges in their hands."[12]

The Union came away with a victory, but at a huge cost in leadership. Major General Jesse L. Reno who commanded the IX Corps, in which the 51st belonged, was killed. The 51st lost 6 men with 22 wounded, none of the casualties coming from John's Company. The Union Army as a whole lost 443 men with 1,807 wounded and 75 missing. The Confederates lost 325 men with 1,560 wounded and 800 missing.

Samuel and the 148th, after receiving uniforms, equipment, and arms left Camp Curtin on the 9th of September heading for Cockeysville, Maryland. There they were detailed to guard sections of the Northern Central Railway from a possible Confederate attack. Samuel's Company was detailed at Jessup's farm near the Gunpowder River. Here the company was divided into "messes," which were basically tents, of 6 men each. They labeled their tents with names such as "Boars Nest," "Dirty Mess," Sheep Mess," and "Turkey Mess." The later more than likely gaining its name from a famous incident of men raiding a farmers turkeys. And because of such antics *"frequent complaints were made to company headquarters by farmers and citizens residing in the vicinity, that foraging parties from Company H had been committing depradations."*[2] It's evident that these young men who came from the same county, and probably knew each other before enlisting, held a special bond. I could not put it better than a member of their company who penned *"Very little selfishness existed among the men in this company, all shoulder to shoulder in common cause, ready to perform any act or face any danger that was presented in common with their brother in arms.*"[2]

While stationed at Cockeysville the 148th lost several men to illness and one man who drowned in the Gunpowder River.

On the 17th of September the bloodiest day in American war history was about to unfold at the Battle of Antietam. After pushing the Confederates back from the fighting at South Mountain, the Union Army caught up with them at Antietam, Maryland. As the Union moved forces toward a strategically located stone bridge to the south of the lines of battle they were stalled. The bridge was locally known as Rohrbach's Bridge, but would be forever known as "Burnside Bridge" after the historic battle fought there.

John and the 51st marched through a cornfield and past a large barn near the bridge. Two previous attempts to cross the bridge by other regiments were bloody failures. Despite heavy losses to the other regiments General Burnside, the new Commanding Officer of the IX Corps, recognized that the bridge must be taken at all costs and ordered the 51st Pennsylvania and 51st New York to storm it a third time – a suicide mission. Colonel John L. Hartranft, the Commanding Officer of the 51st Pennsylvania yelled to his men so that all could hear, *"General Burnside orders the 51st Pennsylvania to storm the bridge!"* At 12:30 in the afternoon Colonel Hartranft led the 51st Pennsylvania to the bridge, passing the dead and wounded from the previous attempts still laying where they fell on the road. As they raced to the bridge and into sight of the Confederates they received volley after volley of rifle and artillery fire from the hillside overlooking the bridge. It must have been as terrifying as it was deadly. As the 51st Pennsylvania ran toward the bridge ahead of the 51st New York, John and his company were leading the way. With men falling at an alarming rate, they pushed on and successfully made it across to secure the other side.

The picture on the following page was taken several days after the battle. This is the perspective John had as he and his comrades ran through the hail of bullets and artillery fire.

Burnside Bridge as it looked in 1862 and viewed as John and the 51st charged it[6]

The bridge was captured and forever immortalize the 51st Pennsylvania with its charge. But the cost was high. The 51st lost 26 men with 106 wounded, 3 captured and 2 deserters. Out of those, John's Company lost Corporal James Dowling along with Privates Miles Dillen, William Wenrick, and Wallis Wiggins. Wounded were Corporal George Armstrong, and Privates William Young, Jacob Casher, George Dutott, Houston Heichel, Robert Hinton, Jesse Lucas, William Maurer, and William Wilson. The three men captured; Privates William Allen, John J. Fisher, and Joseph J. Peters, were all from John's Company.

Also lost that day was Lieutenant Colonel Thomas Bell, a senior member of the 51st. Colonel Hartranft wrote about Bell's death in a letter;

"After crossing the bridge I took the regiment (51st) to the right and halted. When the regiment was re-formed, I moved it from the bed of the road towards the creek, and rested, while several other regiments passed up the road. Colonel Bell here came up to me, saying that more troops should be sent over. I replied 'well, go and see about it.' He went but no further than the bridge, and soon I saw him coming back on the road, (which was now clear of troops,) a few feet from the edge of the road nearest the water. When about thirty yards from the bridge I saw him struck on the left temple, as I at the time thought, and now believe, by a canister shot. He fell backward and rolled off the road to within six feet of the water. He spoke freely, saying 'never say die, boys; 'stand by the colors; 'take care of my sword.' He was immediately taken back to the Barn Hospital and examined by some surgeon, (our own Surgeons being at another hospital,) who pronounced his wound not dangerous. Bleeding soon stopped. I directed Sergeant Major Stoneroad to remain with him and take charge of his effects. I was under orders at this time to move forward, and could not leave the regiment. In little less than an hour after I received permission to go back to the hospital to see the Colonel. I saw him, (Sergeant Major with him) but he did not recognize me. In an hour after he passed off calmly."[1]

On that single day, September 17th, the Union Army lost 2,108 men with 9,540 wounded and 753 captured or missing.

The Confederates lost 1,546 men with 7,752 wounded and 1,018 captured or missing. Many more on both sides later died of wounds received on this bloody day.

The picture on the following page was taken several days after the battle and is viewed from the position the Confederates held overlooking Burnside Bridge.

Burnside Bridge after the battle in 1862 as viewed from the Confederate position[16]

I have visited the Antietam Battlefield on several occasions. Still a rural area in Western Maryland, near the border with Pennsylvania, one gets a somber feeling as you walk the fields where so many men died. Burnside Bridge is located in a beautiful, quiet setting off the beaten path of the normally traveled roads. Not used for much more than a walking trail these days you would never guess the carnage that played out there if it weren't for the monuments placed around it to honor the men that fought and died there.

After the fighting at Burnside Bridge the 51st was relieved and fell back to Pleasant Valley, Maryland where they encamped and recovered. While there John was promoted to corporal on the 1st of October to fill a vacancy caused by that deadly day at Antietam. The promotion brought more responsibility but not an increase in pay, and he continued making $13.00 a month. From the 27th of October until the 19th of November the Union Army and the 51st made their way to Falmouth, Virginia in preparation to take Fredericksburg, Virginia.

Samuel and the 148th were also ordered to proceed to Fredericksburg. Loading up in boxcars they proceeded to Baltimore. There they marched through the city and had a dinner of boiled beef and potatoes, cold ham, bread and coffee, prepared by the Union Relief Association. Then it was on to Washington, DC where they marched through the city with their drum corps playing "Dixie," I assume to indicate that they were heading into the Confederate held south.

The city of Fredericksburg was given the ultimatum of surrendering or it would be shelled and attacked. When there was no reply, and the deadline to respond long overdue, the Union Army shelled the city on the 12th of December. Crossing the Rappahannock River by pontoons the following day John and the 51st found themselves moving through the streets of Fredericksburg headed toward an area known as Marye's Heights.

Fredericksburg as John viewed it before crossing the Rappahannock River[18]

This area overlooked the city and was heavily fortified by the Confederates. As soon as the 51st emerged from the streets of Fredericksburg they were blasted by enemy fire. *"The men of the 51st P.V. were falling at every step and men were laying weltering in their gore all around, some killed outright, some with legs and arms torn off, many with headless bodies. The sight was terrible in the extreme."*[12]

Holding their position they fought until dark and used the shelled out houses in the city as a defensive position. After 3 days of holding their position, and not making any progress, John and the regiment fell back across the Rappahannock River. Once back on the other side outside the reach of

Confederate artillery they set up camp with the rest of the Union force

Shelled out houses in Fredericksburg that John and the 51st used as a defensive position[6]

During the battle the 51st lost 14 men with 78 wounded, 2 missing, and 1 deserter. John's Company had 4 men wounded; Sergeant William Hichel, and Privates William Recides, James Beightol, and George Meisse.

The Confederates had held their ground and scored a victory at Fredericksburg. During the battle the Union lost 1,284 men with 9,600 wounded and 1,769 captured or missing. The Confederates lost 608 men with 4,116 wounded and 653 captured or missing.

Samuel and the 148th did not cross the Potomac River until the 16th of December and didn't arrive in Falmouth until the 18th, well after the Battle of Fredericksburg was over.

An interesting side story to the battles fought at Second Bull Run, Antietam and Fredericksburg by John and the 51st was that in all cases they went up against a young Confederate Calvary officer by the name of John C. Pelham. Pelham had been attending the United States Military Academy at West Point when the war was heating up. Wanting to fight he resigned his commission and returned to his home state of Alabama to fight for the Confederacy. A young and highly skilled artillery officer he was known for his extreme bravery. Unfortunately, he lost his life at the Battle of Kelly's Ford near Culpeper, Virginia on the 17th of March 1863.

I was struck when I came across his name because in 1982 while serving in the United States Army I was attached to the 2nd Infantry Division in South Korea, near the demilitarized zone. The camp I was assigned to for my one year tour of duty was named "John C. Pelham," in honor of the late Confederate officer.

It seems that, at least in my immediate family, the legacy of Confederate officers has crossed paths with John's descendant's more than Union officers.

1863

After the defeat at Fredericksburg the 51st remained in the area to participate in another offensive that never did materialize. Subsequently they marched to Aquia Creek and on the 9th of February boarded the steamer *Louisiana*. The following day John and the 51st were back at Fortress Monroe, Virginia.

The Union IX Corps boarding vessels at Aquia Creek, Virginia bound for Fortress Monroe[16]

While at Fortress Monroe on the 14th of February the 1 year anniversary of the Battle of New Berne was honored with a single ration of whiskey for each man. I'm not sure if John was a drinker, but if not I'm sure his ration did not go to waste. On the 20th of March John was promoted to 1st Sergeant to fill the vacancy of Sergeant George Campbell who was promoted to 2nd Lieutenant on the 11th of January. The added responsibility came with a pay raise and John was now making $20.00 a month.

Meanwhile Samuel and the 148th were still at Falmouth where they had wintered over and established a picket line. The weather was very cold and Samuel was sick in quarters over most of January and February. It's possible that he had contracted Typhoid Fever, although not documented, because men in his regiment were known to have been sick with it. In fact two men in Samuel's Company died from Typhoid Fever; Private Thomas Gephart on the 5th of March and Private Amos Sweetland on the 1st of April.

John and the 51st packed up and boarded the steamer *Kennebec* in Newport News, Virginia on the 26th of March. In transit John and the regiment enjoyed playing cards and dancing with each other to help pass the time. The following day they arrived in Baltimore and boarded a train which took them to Pittsburgh, Pennsylvania and then on to Paris, Kentucky, arriving there on the 1st of April. From Paris they marched through blinding snow to the outskirts of Mount Sterling, Kentucky where they set up camp. While there, John's

Company was detailed with several others from the regiment to provide security for the nearby town of Winchester, Kentucky.

Leaving Falmouth on the 27th of April Samuel and the 148th, along with a large Union force, were ordered south to Chancellorsville, Virginia. Four days later they were about a half a mile away from Chancellorsville when they ran into the enemy. This would be the first time Samuel and the 148th engaged the enemy in battle. From the 1st to the 2nd the regiment skirmished with the Confederates and due to heavy artillery bombardments dug in for protection. The two armies fought each other fiercely for several days without the 148th really being involved as they were positioned toward the rear. But when the regiments that were fighting on the front line drifted back through the 148th's line, the horrors of battle started to sink in as the wounded and shattered passed them seeking treatment. As the forward Union regiments fell back, the 148th moved forward into what would be considered the second bloodiest day in American history, after the Battle of Antietam.

At 0800 on the 3rd of May, companies D, C, G, and H - Samuel's Company, were ordered to attack. As they left their protected positions, carrying the regiment's colors, they marched double time passing behind the Chancellor House and in front of the Bullock House before entering dense woods and brush. The brush was so thick they were unaware that the enemy front line was only 20 yards to their right until the Confederates opened up with a full volley, catching them by surprise. As Samuel entered the brush with Private Thomas

Myton and the rest of H Company, Myton described what happened and the carnage going on around him;

"Immediately the air seemed full of bullets and one passing through the side of a small tree struck me on the right shoulder, cutting my knapsack strap about half off, seriously bruising the flesh and slightly cutting the skin. The blow seemed serious and for a time I thought my collar bone was broken. Just then orders came to lie down and fire. I turned to leave the line but thought I had better be sure I had sufficient excuse for going. I found no bones were broken and that my arm worked all right and I returned to the front and began to fire. We had struck their line obliquely giving them a flank fire on us. The fire from the front was low but the fire from the angle was direct and deadly. Coming through the woods I was losing faith in myself because of a certain nervousness and a disposition of my knees to knock together, but now my gun came down steadily, and I observed that I was doing good shooting and began to be on better terms with myself. The distance was very short; not more than forty yards, I think, and the fighting became fast and furious. In order to facilitate rapid firing I did not return my rammer to the thembels but laid it by my knee. This had continued for some time when as I turned my head to put a cap on the nipple of my gun, a rifle ball struck me in the lower part of my nose and through my upper lip. I put my hand to my face and it felt as if my nose and upper lip were torn to shreds. I uttered a soldier's prayer and took up my gun to kill somebody but the benevolent enterprise was frustrated by the blood from my wound running into my mouth.

I turned to leave the field and thought it was safer to creep under their fire than to attempt to walk through it, but the first step I took, a bullet passed through my left arm above the elbow shattering the bone, and I fell on my side, fortunately, with my shoulder behind a small tree, into which two or three bullets struck and bounced out against my side. I decided it was safer to lie where I was than to attempt to get out, and for what seemed to me a very long time, I lay there. The experience of that interval lying there fully exposed to that fire with the consciousness that any second might be my last, and fully expecting it, I shall never forget. It may be imagined but can never be described. After what seemed a long time the firing slackened about me and I looked up, our line was falling back. I saw Bob Cassidy (Big Bob) taking aim from side of a tree and making a very wry face as he prepared to shoot some one. I felt drowsiness coming over me and passed into unconsciousness. I do not know how long I remained so, but when I became conscious again, the fighting was over and everything quiet. I rose to my feet and essayed to start to the rear, the first step I took I placed my foot in a pool of blood (presumably my own) my foot slipped throwing me forward, drawing my knapsack violently over my bruised shoulder and setting my broken arm to swinging and the broken bones to grinding together. The pain was intense, beads of perspiration broke out on my face and I became totally blind, my knapsack seemed to be pulling me back, I had the sense of falling backward. I was in the 'valley of the shadow' and alone. The thought came to me that if I fell I should die there, and with all the strength I had left I bent my foot forward until my knapsack was over my feet and waited, in total darkness. Presently I began to see by distorted vision, saw men as trees walking, but I waited patiently and after some time everything assumed its normal shape. Remembering the trouble with my knapsack I unslung it and lifted it from my left shoulder, passed it down gently over my broken arm and laid it on the ground. As it rested on the ground I observed at my feet and so near where I had lain that I could easily have laid my hand on his face, the body of Michael Flinn. His fair young face half buried in the brown dead leaves, apparently he had died in peace and without much pain."[2]

The fighting continued for 3 hours until 1100 when the 4 companies of the 148th were relieved. Shattered they fell back to their protected position with the rest of the regiment. Of the men that entered the brush over half were killed or wounded. One witness said *"It seemed as they fell back that there were more men left on the line of battle then were relieved."*[2] They eventually withdraw with the rest of the Union force as they conceded from the battlefield.

Declared a Confederate victory it came at a steep price. The Confederates lost 1,665 men with 9,081 wounded and 2,018 captured or missing. Including one of their most prominent and beloved officers, General Thomas "Stonewall" Jackson, who was wounded and died several days later. The Union lost 1,606 men with 9,672 wounded and 5,919 captured or missing.

View of the woods and brush at Chancellorsville showing the trees cut by artillery shells[6]

The 148th lost 31 men with 119 wounded and 14 missing. Samuel's Company lost 7; Corporal Matthew B. Lucas, along with Privates Michael Flinn, William Ludwig, Wyraman S. Miller, James M. Test, Ulysses Wants, and Harrison Yeager. There were 22 wounded; Captain George A. Bayard, Lieutenants John L. Johnston and John A. Bayard, Corporals Richard Miles and George H. Neiman, Privates William H. Close, John W. Gahagan, Francis J. Hunter, George T. Jones, George H. Long, Michael Lebkecher, Thomas W. Myton,

William Orris, Frederick Reeder, Charles O. Wipps, Danial W. Woodring, Adoniram Yothers, William Lucas, Oscar Runk, Daniel Farley, Jacob Frantz, and Benjamin Zimmerman. Privates Reeder and Zimmerman later died from their wounds. Corporal Miles and Privates Lebkecker, Hunter, Myton, Yothers, and Woodring each had an arm amputated.

After receiving his facial wound H Company's Commanding Officer, Captain George Bayard, made his way to the field hospital to have it treated properly and check on his men. There he found a grizzly sight of them suffering and dying, with their amputated arms and legs piled on the ground. He was witnessing, along with Samuel and the rest of the 148th, the cruel reality of war. From here the 148th fell back to Falmouth and awaited its next assignment.

John and the 51st started to move south on the 4th of June. After numerous marches, train rides, and a river boat ride on the Mississippi River they arrived at Milldale, Mississippi on the 17th. There they were tasked with digging rifle pits and clearing woods, protecting the rear during the siege of Vicksburg, Mississippi.

Union fortifications at Vicksburg, Missisippi[6]

On the 14th of June, Samuel and the 148th broke camp and headed back north arriving in Uniontown, Maryland on the 30th. The following day, probably the most well-known of all the Civil War battles commenced in Gettysburg, Pennsylvania. The battle lasted for three days and recorded the most casualties of any of the battles fought during the war. Furthermore, it was fought on Pennsylvania soil and must have had a personal meaning to the men of 148th. Only 130 miles from his hometown of Snow Shoe, Samuel knew he was fighting to protect his family.

It was said many years later by a veteran of the 148th that the men of the regiment showed they knew how to die at Chancellorsville but at Gettysburg they showed they knew how to fight.

On the 1st of July Samuel and the 148th marched almost 16 miles and encamped about 2 miles from Gettysburg. In the morning they were up early and marched to the right of Little Round Top and took up a position to the left of Cemetery Hill, on the Hummelbough farm. At 1600 Samuel and the 148th were ordered to advance through a wheatfield. As they crossed the wheatfield the Confederates poured volley after volley at the advancing Union force and the bullets were coming at the 148th *"as thick as fallen hail."*[2] Pushing on they were able to drive the Confederates from their position. But eventually Samuel and the 148th had to retrace their steps back through the wheatfield as the Confederates counter attacked. The wheatfield would change hands 6 times before dark when it was eventually controlled by the Confederates. After falling back the 148th had rejoined the main Union battle line where they spent the night protecting an artillery battery.

On the morning of the 3rd of July all was quiet as Samuel and the 148th watched the Confederates prepare their men and artillery for an attack. At 1300 the Confederates initiated their charge with an artillery barrage, which was promptly answered by Union artillery. The thunderous exchange was so intense that Samuel and the regiment hugged the ground for protection.

And then came the attack which would be forever known as "Pickett's Charge," in name of one of the Confederate General's leading the charge, George Pickett;

"About seventeen thousand men who had formed for this charge in the rear of their works in the edge of the woods

three-fourths of a mile away, made their appearance in our front. Emerging from the woods in three long double lines of battle, they moved out over their works in splendid style. From the location of our Regiment we could see the first double line across their works, then came a second and a third line. The long lines of gray moved across the fields toward us in perfect order. Berdan's sharpshooters commenced firing, picking out their officers – their globe sighted guns being effective at long range. Soon our artillery along the line of the cemetery to the Little Round Top opened on them with shells, grape and canister, and when their lines reached the Emmitsburg Road, our infantry commenced firing at short range. The effect was terrible. Great gaps were opened in their lines by our cannon balls……Then came the hand to hand conflict……when pistols, swords, bayonets, butts of muskets and ramrods were freely used. This lasted only a few moments, when the Johnnies commenced to throw down their arms and surrender, over four hundred prisoners coming in over the breastworks of the 148th Regiment. Great was the rejoicing over the victory."[2]

The battle took a toll on Samuel as he was wounded in the right hip during the fighting on the 2nd of July. Reported as a slight wound it's not known if it was deemed bad enough to remove him from the battlefield at the time. It seems a ball (bullet) went through his torso just above his right hip and exited about an inch from his spine. It is never stated where in the battle he was wounded but the heaviest fighting on the 2nd was done at the infamous "Wheatfield."

Casualty Sheet for Samuel's wound at Gettysburg

When the fighting was over the 148th held their position that looked out over the massive carnage that resulted from three days of fierce fighting. This was only the second battle Samuel and the 148th had been in and they both would rank with the deadliest of the war.

The Union Army was victorious and the battle was arguably the turning point of the war. The Confederate Army entered Gettysburg on the offensive and deep into Union territory. Now the Union Army went on the offensive and began to push the Confederates back into the south. The changing tide of Gettysburg, the bloodiest battle of the Civil War, cost the Union 3,155 men with 14,531 wounded and 5,369 captured or missing. The Confederates lost 4,708 men with 12,693 wounded and 5,830 captured or missing.

The 148th recorded 27 killed, 93 wounded, and 5 captured or missing. Out of these Samuel's Company lost Sergeant Samuel M'Kinley and Private James Stewart. Wounded were 2nd Lieutenant John A. Bayard and Privates James E. Beals, John Green, Edward P. Jones, and Samuel Gunsallus. Of these Bayard, Beals, and Green all died of their wounds in just over a month.

The company was hard hit with the loss of 2nd Lieutenant Bayard who was the son of H Company's Commanding Officer, Captain Bayard. A member of the company who helped carry him to the field hospital said; *"I went to the hospital and stayed all night with him, gave him water and did all I could to make him comfortable, while I was with him he never murmured or complained or showed any signs of suffering, although he knew his wound was mortal."*[2] He died on the 1st of August.

The dead awaiting burial at the Wheatfield[16]

There are two monuments in the Gettysburg National Military Park dedicated to the 148th. One is at the Wheatfield and the other nearby where they later fell back in the evening of the 2nd to provide cover for an artillery regiment. I have been to see both and visited the entire battlefield and town of Gettysburg on many occasions. The Park Service does a tremendous job there, as with all Civil War sites, keeping the battlefield looking as it did in 1863. Many of the original farm houses and city buildings are still standing. Some bear the scars of cannonball and bullet holes. Probably the most memorable time I visited the battlefield was in the fall when my wife and I took a horseback tour with some friends. Riding through the fields and along pathways everyone was silent and the only sound was that of horses' hooves beating the ground as we rode along. The crisp air blew across the wheat and cornfields and brought with it a sobering realization of just what had occurred on these hallowed grounds. It was very moving.

On the 4th of July as Samuel and the 148th held their position at Gettysburg, John and the 51st were over a thousand miles away watching the fall of Vicksburg. Pushing east through Vicksburg the 51st was brought up with a Union force to advance on Jackson, Mississippi.

After Gettysburg the 148th started to follow the Confederate Army as they retreated. But the wound Samuel sustained was serious enough for him to be sent to McKim's Hospital in Baltimore, Maryland. Samuel doesn't state how he made it to McKim's Hospital but Private Robert M. Wadding of I Company described his own experience and it was likely similar to Samuel's since they arrived there about the same time; *"Our company here being in the wheat field, with another or so of our regiment on our right suffering terribly. I here received a bad gunshot wound in my groin, obliging me to remain there till the battle was over……..After lying on the earth for fifteen days I, with hundreds of others was removed to Baltimore in freight cars, we lay on straw or hay on the floor of the car. I was taken in to McKim's Hospital."*[2]

With over 27,000 men wounded on both sides you can imagine how chaotic the aid stations and local hospitals were after the battle. As Private Wadding states he waited 15 days to be sent to a hospital. He and Samuel were lucky to make it to

McKim's as many men died waiting on the ground or battlefield to be treated.

Medical Descriptive List for Samuel at McKim's Hospital

As John and the 51st moved toward Jackson, Mississippi they skirmished daily with the Confederates, losing one man to an accidental death and 4 wounded by enemy fire.

On the 11th of July they arrived outside of Jackson, Mississippi and were placed to the north of the city on the left of the Union line, all the while under a constant artillery bombardment.

At 0800 the following morning they engaged the enemy and a heavy artillery barrage was exchanged. The fighting was close and the 51st dug in for protection forward of the Union line, which they were told to hold at all costs. On the 14th they were relieved and pulled back beyond the Insane Asylum, just north of the city. Three days later the 51st were called back to the front for the assault on Jackson and the city was taken. John and his regiment were the first in the city and raised their colors in the yard of the Capital Building.

It was a Union victory but the battle cost them 100 men with 800 wounded and 100 missing. The Confederates lost 71 men with 504 wounded and 764 missing. Although the 51st reported taking casualties in an "after-action report" I could not find any mention of killed or wounded in their muster rolls.

You may have noticed in these battles that there are a lot of men listed as "missing." These figures usually came from the official record of each army and were tabulated just after the battle. Most of the missing usually turned out later to have been killed in action. In the rush to bury the dead many men were unidentifiable due to severe wounds or they had no identification. To compound matters marked graves were usually identified by a piece of wood that didn't last long and the identity of the occupant was eventually lost to history.

On the 20th of July the 51st was marching west back toward Vicksburg and arrived at their previous position before the siege of Vicksburg along the Mississippi River. Here they commenced to digging trenches for a defensive fortification.

Surprisingly life for John and his regiment was very comfortable here. Granted the intense heat of a southern summer had its drawbacks. But they were able to forage fresh fruit that was in season and had established a bakery that made fresh bread and pies.

But the war was still being fought in other parts of the country and on the 10th of August the 51st packed up and boarded the steamer *Emerald* and headed north up the Mississippi River. Arriving at Cairo, Illinois 4 days later they boarded railroad cars of the Illinois Central Railroad. While the train, which consisted of 12 cars, made its way to Cincinnati, Ohio it derailed near Shoals, Indiana on the 16th. The accident sent two cars tumbling down an embankment killing 2 men and injuring 9. By the following day the regiment had the train righted and back in motion, arriving in Cincinnati on the 18th of August. They made camp outside of the city for a few days then marched to Nicholasville, Kentucky and then on to Crab Orchard, Kentucky. While at Crab Orchard the 51st cast their votes for the Governor of Pennsylvania and the results were 208 for the incumbent, Republican Andrew Curtin, and 28 for the challenger, Democrat George Woodward. Since John was a staunch Republican all of his life[9] I'm sure he cast his ballot for Curtin, who was the eventual winner. From Crab Orchard the regiment slowly made their way south to just outside of Knoxville, Tennessee.

Samuel was released from McKim's Hospital on the 22nd of September and rejoined the 148th in the vicinity of Rappahannock, Virginia as they guarded the railyards there.

On the 13th of October the regiment moved with a Union force to Auburn, Virginia where the 148th acted as rear guard protecting the railways during an engagement with the Confederates. The skirmish at Auburn didn't decide much and neither side sustained more than a few casualties, none affecting the 148th. After the skirmish the 148th received 125 men as replacements on the 29th of October and 10 days later 158 more were added bringing them back to full strength.

Starting on the 12th of October Samuel and the 148th got into a string of skirmishes with the Confederates in Northern Virginia. The first being at Rappahannock Station, then Auburn Mills, and finally Briscoe Station. The 148th along with other Union forces were shadowing the Confederates and skirmished with them as they moved north. Casualties were light on both side and 2 men were reported wounded with the 148th.

November found Samuel and the 148th bumping heads with the Confederates south of the Rappahannock River at Kelly's Ford on the 7th and Mine Run on the 27th. These were also minor skirmishes and once again resulted in few casualties.

On the 15th of November John and the 51st were on the move heading south to Campbell's Station, Tennessee. This was the location of a strategic railroad junction through which essential supplies were transported into Knoxville. The Confederates realizing its importance as well, made a dash for the rail junction. The weather was miserable with heavy rains turning the roads thick with mud. The artillery was having a tough time making any headway, with their heavy guns sinking into the mud, and the 51st was tasked with assisting them. The following day the Union force reached Campbell's Station first and set up and a defensive position across Kingston and Louden Roads. About fifteen minutes later the Confederates arrived, and the fighting began. As the Union force held off the Confederate attack, Union trains were moved through Campbell's Station to resupply Knoxville. As darkness fell, and the Confederates poured into the area, the Union force pulled back into the safety of a fortified and now well supplied Knoxville.

The fighting at Campbell's Station was considered a Union victory because they were able to get their trains through the junction and resupply Knoxville. There were about 450 casualties on each side with the 51st sustained 7 wounded - 2 mortally. John's Company was unhurt.

The 51st remained in Knoxville defending the city and immediately commenced building fortifications and preparing for an attack. Artillery shelling went back and forth during the 14 day siege and the 51st lost 2 men, 4 wounded and 1 captured. In John's Company Private Robert Hinton was wounded twice.

Even though they had the city surrounded the Confederates elected to wait for reinforcements before conducting a full scale attack. Eventually they realized that they had wasted away their opportunity and fell back. But the siege was rough on the Union occupiers who had quickly used up their food supplies. *"During the hardship of the siege the men had been compelled to subsist on meagre rations of a quality hardly capable of sustaining life."*[1]

As the Confederates pulled back the Union force began to pursue them. Even though the Confederates were on the run the managed to inflict damage. On the 15th of December the Confederates captured 4 men along with a wagon train meant to resupply John's regiment with food. This was a heavy blow to the 51st as they had been suffering from low provisions since the siege. And two days later they skirmished with a Confederate Cavalry regiment and Private George Meisse of John's Company was wounded.

John and The 51st found themselves ending the year camped about 18 miles from Knoxville where they had skirmished with the Confederate Cavalry. Still very low on food they were normally only issued two crackers a day. Typically the regiment foraged from the land to sustain themselves. But in mid-December there were no crops or wild food to forage from. And the Confederates had made sure any livestock were seized or destroyed as they marched ahead of them.

After the skirmish at Mine Run, Samuel and the 148th had moved to Stevensburg, Virgina where they wintered over at Hansbrough's Ridge until February.

1864

In January the original men of the 51st were coming up on the end of their 3 year enlistment. As an incentive to re-enlist each man was offered a bounty and the entire regiment was awarded a 30 day Veterans Furlough home. At this point in the war John could have walked away with no questions asked. Some in his regiment did walk away. With all the death and destruction these men had witnessed over the past 3 years no one would blame them.

But John and many of his regimental comrades did re-enlist. Out of the original 100 or so men that started with John in G Company 22 re-enlisted. It's not to say that the remainder decided to walk away, as some did, but the company had also lost a good number of the original men to sickness, wounds, and death.

John's bounty to re-enlist was $400. He was paid $60 up front with the balance of $340 spread out over his re-enlistment. After committing themselves for another 3 years the regiment headed home for their 30 day furlough. John and the 51st broke camp on the 18th of January in a blinding snow storm and commenced their journey home via Cincinnati, Ohio and then on to Harrisburg. Although a majority of the journey was by railroad it was stated that each man wore out a pair of shoes for all the ground they had to cover marching home.

The regiment arrived back in Harrisburg on the 9th of February and they were greeted with a hero's welcome. The men of the 51st were so popular back in Pennsylvania that they easily recruited to fill the regiment back to capacity. I assume John used his furlough to go home and spend time with his parents and siblings.

During this time he would have surely spoken with his younger brother Taylor about his experiences in the war. Taylor was 16 years old, of fair complexion, dark hair, and 6ft tall - which was very tall for the period. If John tried to deter him from joining the fight it didn't work. Taylor had already tried to sign up with H Company of the 46th Regiment Infantry, Pennsylvania Volunteers on the 29th of June 1863. He later mustered-in with the regiment on the 15th of July 1863 in Huntington, Pennsylvania. But I think because of his age, which was 16 at the time, he was discharged just 4 days later. The age to enlist was 18 years old, but you could enlist at a younger age with your parent's signed consent. His Parents already had two sons in the war and I can't image they were willing to send their youngest son off any sooner than they had to.

Taylor was persistent and apparently did not want to leave the fighting up to his brothers because he made another under aged attempt to enlist. This time he traveled to Hollidaysburg, Pennsylvania which is about 60 miles south of Snow Shoe.

I assume he did this because no one would know him that far from home and he could get away with lying about his age. When enlisting Taylor stated his age as 19 years, but he was actually 17 years and 2 months. I also don't think he could write, although the 1860 Census states he had attended school within the past year. I make this assumption because he didn't sign his name to his enlistment contract, but placed an "X" as his mark.

This time he was successful and mustered-in with M Company of the 13th Regiment, Pennsylvania Cavalry on the 8th of March 1864. Like Samuel he was now making $13.00 a month as a private. And he received a substantial bounty in the amount of $300.00, which was spread out over his enlistment. That was well over 2 years of pay and a mighty big incentive to lie about your age to join.

The 13th Cavalry was already well established and battle hardened by the time young Taylor joined. The regiment had been initially formed as the 116th Pennsylvania "Irish Dragoons" and was to be attached to a New York unit in 1861. But due to state mandated regimental quotas the unit was reformed as the 13th Regiment, Pennsylvania Cavalry in 1862.

VOLUNTEER ENLISTMENT.

STATE OF _Pennsylvania_ **TOWN OF** _Hollidaysburg_

I, _Taylor Funsalous_ born in _Centre Co_, in the State of _Pennsylvania_, aged _Nineteen_ years, and by occupation a _Farmer_, Do HEREBY ACKNOWLEDGE to have volunteered this _Eighth_ day of _March_ 186_4_ to serve as a **Soldier** in the **Army of the United States of America**, for the period of THREE YEARS, unless sooner discharged by proper authority: Do also agree to accept such bounty, pay, rations, and clothing, as are, or may be, established by law for volunteers. And I, _Taylor Funsalous_ do solemnly swear, that I will bear true faith and allegiance to the **United States of America**, and that I will serve them honestly and faithfully against all their enemies or opposers whomsoever; and that I will observe and obey the orders of the President of the United States, and the orders of the officers appointed over me, according to the Rules and Articles of War.

Sworn and subscribed to, at _Hollidaysburg_
this _8th_ day of _March_, 186_ _.   _Taylor_ x _Funsallus_
BEFORE _Henry N Baker Lt 156 Regt_   his mark

I CERTIFY, ON HONOR, That I have carefully examined the above-named Volunteer, agreeably to the General Regulations of the Army, and that, in my opinion, he is free from all bodily defects and mental infirmity, which would in any way disqualify him from performing the duties of a soldier.

A. Rothrock
Surgeon B'd enrolment
EXAMINING SURGEON.

I CERTIFY, ON HONOR, That I have minutely inspected the Volunteer, _Taylor Funsolus_, previously to his enlistment, and that he was entirely sober when enlisted; that, to the best of my judgment and belief, he is of lawful age; and that, in accepting him as duly qualified to perform the duties of an able-bodied soldier, I have strictly observed the Regulations which govern the recruiting service. This soldier has _Grey_ eyes, _Dark_ hair, _Fair_ complexion, is _Five_ feet _Six_ inches high.

Henry N Baker Lt
_13th_ Regiment of _Pa Cav_ Volunteers,
RECRUITING OFFICER.

(A. G. O. No. 74 & 76.)

Taylor's enlistment contract

DECLARATION OF RECRUIT.

I, Taylor Gunsollus, desiring to VOLUNTEER as a Soldier in the Army of the United States, for the term of THREE YEARS, Do Declare, That I am ninteen years and _____ months of age; that I have never been discharged from the United States service on account of disability or by sentence of a court martial, or by order before the expiration of a term of enlistment; and I know of no impediment to my serving honestly and faithfully as a soldier for three years.

GIVEN at Wallis Mays Burg the 8th day of November 1864.

Witness: J. S. Altee

Taylor X Gunsallus
       mark

Volunteered at Wallisburg, March 8th, 1864, by Lieut. N. Boyles, 13th Regiment of Cavalry.

No. 911

Taylor Gunsallus

Discharged from 13th Penn Cavalry

Reg't of _____ 18__.

enlistment (last servied in Company ( )

CONSENT IN CASE OF MINOR.

I, _____ DO CERTIFY, That I am the _____ of _____; that the said _____ is _____ years of age; and I do hereby freely give my CONSENT to his volunteering as a SOLDIER in the ARMY OF THE UNITED STATES for the period of THREE YEARS.

GIVEN at _____ the _____ day of _____

Witness:

(A. G. O. No. 74 & 75.)

Taylor's enlistment contract, second page

With all that John had witness over the past 3 years I can only imagine the mixed feelings he had when he learned his baby brother had joined the fight.

While back home in Pennsylvania the 51st was hailed with great fan fair. Being at home must have been a huge relief after almost 3 long years of army life. But there was still a war going on and John and his regiment formed back up at Camp Curtin in Harrisburg on the 10th of March. Leaving on the 20th the regiment arrived back in Annapolis, Maryland the following day. Here they continued to drill and prepare for the next campaign. Anxious to leave cool and rainy Maryland the regiment was now attached to the 3rd Division of IX Corps and started to head south on the 24th of April. Their destination was an area known as the Wilderness, near Chancellorsville and Spotsylvania, Virginia.

Meanwhile, Samuel and the 148th were detailed to the II Corps and also headed to the Wilderness. And Samuel's company would once again be *"called to make sacrifices that seemed out of all proportion to the advantage that could reasonably be expected to be derived from the movement."*[2]

Taylor mustered-in with the 13th Cavalry on or about the 16th of April as they were performing picket duty around Bristoe Station, Virginia. On the 3rd of May the 13th Cavalry was detailed to the 4th Division of IX Corps and like his brothers, Taylor headed to the Wilderness.

Converging on the Confederates the three brothers were heading into the back to back Battles of the Wilderness from the 4th to 7th and Spotsylvania from the 8th to the 21st.

Taylor and the 13th Cavalry crossed the Rapidan River at Germanna Ford on the 4th of May followed by John and the 51st the following day. Both John and Taylor were headed toward the Wilderness Tavern.

The Union Army along with Taylor and the 13th Pennsylvania Cavalry crossing the Rapidan River at Germanna Ford on the 4th of May 1864[20]

Samuel and the 148th crossed the Rapidan River further east at Ely's Ford on the 4th and headed toward Chancellorsville.

The Battle of the Wilderness *"was fought in the midst of dense thickets of second-growth underbrush, evergreens, pines, sweet-gums, scrub-oak, and cedar, rendering the use of artillery impossible, and compelling the opposing lines to approach very near each other in order to see their opponents. It was simply a series of fierce attacks and repulses on either side, and the contending lines swayed back and forth over a strip of ground from 300 yards to 2 miles in width, on which the wounded of both sides were scattered, and to add to the horror the woods was on fire in many places, and a great many of the wounded, who were unable to escape, were thus either suffocated or burned to death."*[12] *"The screams of the dying men echoed for a long time in the minds of the men who fought there."*[10]

John and the 51st made contact with the enemy on the 6th of May. While scouting for the Confederate line the 51st was the first regiment of their division to engage and subsequently led the rest of the division in to their location. But as the regiment advanced and took the Confederate fortification the rest of the division failed to cover their flank and the 51st had to give back some hard fought ground. As the day drew to a close the division reformed on the 51st's flank and the fortification was retaken.

View of the Confederate entrenchments and woods at the Battle of the Wilderness[19]

The fighting in the dense woods went back and forth for several days. The 51st lost 11 men with 79 wounded, 5 captured, and 1 deserter. John's Company lost Corporal John E. Wilt and Private Aaron Thatcher with Privates George Dutot and William Heichel wounded.

At the same time Samuel and the 148th were fighting just south of the 51st on the other side of Orange Plank Road. They were looking for a place to join the Union front line but ended up toward the rear and only lost 1 man with 2 men wounded.

Taylor and the 13th Cavalry engaged the enemy near Guinea Station but did not sustain any casualties.

As the battle subsided the Union had lost 2,246 men with 12,037 wounded and 3,383 missing or captured. The Confederates lost 1,477 men with 7,866 wounded and 1,690 missing or captured. The battle was a draw and both armies immediately regrouped for the next engagement.

By the 9th of May John's 51st, Samuel's 148th, and Taylor's 13th Cavalry had pulled back to the Ni River where they regrouped.

The following morning the 148th moved toward Po River, Virginia as the Battle of Spotsylvania was unfolding. A Confederate force emerged from some woods and charged the regiment. Samuel's Company was the first to engage them with a strong volley, followed by the rest of the regiment. The Confederates then pulled back to a defensive position and inflicted heavy casualties on the exposed 148th.

Unknown to the 148th other Union forces that had been supporting them had pulled back and left one of their flanks exposed to enemy fire, which was a huge tactical error. To make matters worse their other flank, which was heavy woods, had caught fire from exploding artillery shells. The commanding officer of the 148th wrote their situation *was "the most critical in which the Regiment was placed during the War."*[2] And it could have been disastrous, with the regiment being totally wiped out. But cool heads prevailed and the regiment pulled back safely to a defensive position.

The fighting went on until night fall when Samuel and the 148th were pulled back to rejoin the rest of the Union force. Po River alone left the 148th with 21 men dead, 79 wounded and 1 captured. Samuel's Company lost Private Isaac Sweetwood while Lieutenant James B. Cook and Corporal William McDonald were mortally wounded. Wounded were Corporal John D. Wagner and Privates William H. Kellerman, Samuel M. Moyer, Jacob Bracken, Darius L. Sanders, Frederick Shaffer, Valentine Stonebraker, Irvin Lowry, Joseph Lape, and Henry Johnston. Corporal Ephraim Klinger was captured.

The battle raged on over the 11th of May as Union forces probed the Confederate lines. Then on the 12th John's 51st and Samuel's 148th were ordered to attack a heavily fortified position called the "Salient," or what was later known as the "Bloody Angle." This was where the fiercest fighting took place trying to break through the Confederate line. As a heavy rain fell Samuel's 148th was one of the lead regiments to hit the enemy line and enter their trenches. Hand to hand combat ensued. The first line was taken and as they passed on to the next line a member of the regiment described what he saw; *"Accustomed as we were, to the scenes of blood and carnage, the spectacle inside the intrenchments was sickening. The ghastly faces of the dead and their mangled bodies piled in the traverses bore awful testimony to the deadly effect of our rifles and bayonets."*[2]

As they reached the second set of defenses the Confederates continued to put up a hard fight and the 148th were driven back to the first set of defenses. Here they withstood a tremendous Confederate counterattack trying to regain their fortifications. The fighting was beyond the scope of anything the 148th had ever seen. *"Words can give no adequate idea of the dreadful sanguinary conflict. Hour after hour, all day long men grappled over the works in bloody struggle. They fired their guns full in each other's faces. They lunged at each other with bayonet thrust. They leaped upon the works and fired down among the maddened crowd on the other side. They grappled in mortal combat to wrest flags from each other. They held their guns overhead and shot downward into the enemy. Hour after hour, all day long, they fought like demons. It was a literal saturnalia of blood. It was grim visaged war in full panoply of horror."*[2]

As Samuel and his company charged the line head on, in what his commanding officer said *"was unquestionably the most successful bayonet charge of the War,"*[2] John and the 51st were attacking it to the left. But John did not make the same penetration that his brother and the 148th had made. As John got to within a few hundred yards of the "Bloody Angle" the 51st were hit with heavy artillery and rifle fire, which drove them to take cover behind a dirt embankment. But having their flank once again exposed, the Confederates charged upon them and the engagement turned to hand to hand combat. The fighting was so unbelievably close and overwhelming for the 51st that many men surrendered and two of their battle flags were captured. Although severely overwhelmed by the situation John and the 51st held their ground.

Having the battle flag – or regimental colors, captured was humiliating to a regiment on both sides of the fighting. And obtaining an enemy's flag was not an easy task because they were protected at all costs. Two men in Samuel's 148th were awarded the Medal of Honor - the United States' highest military award for capturing Confederate flags during the Battle of Spotsylvania. They were Privates Robert W. Ammerman and George W. Harris.

The day ran the gambit of honor and defeat. And alas it also turned deadly for the Gunsallus brothers. The fierce fighting at the "Bloody Angle" claimed the life of 23 year old Samuel. It's not known how he died, but knowing how horrific the fighting was at the "Bloody Angle" I pray it was a quick death.

Samuel's date of death is a bit confusing. He is officially listed on his Death Certificate as being killed on the 16th of May. But the official Casualty Sheet from the 148th, just after the battle, has his death occurring on the 14th. And the letter to his family from the Adjutant General's Office gives the date of his death as the 10th. However his comrades in H Company say he was killed in the assault on the 12th. I will side with his comrades who were there with him fighting at the "Bloody Angle."

Due to the massive confusion of war and the necessity to bury the dead quickly, Samuel was first buried at McCoull's Farm in Spotsylvania along with 1,492 other Union soldiers. His comrades state he was buried in an *"unknown grave."*[2] But he was later exhumed, identified, and moved to his current location at the Fredericksburg National Cemetery in Virginia.

McCoull's Farm house where Samuel was initially buried[19]

CASUALTY SHEET.

Name: Samuel Junsatius
Rank: Private   Company: "H"   Regiment: 148"
Arm: Infty   State: Pennsylvania
Nature of Casualty: Death

CAUSE OF CASUALTY—(Name of Disease, &c.)

BY WHOM DISCHARGED

FROM WHAT SOURCE THIS INFORMATION WAS OBTAINED.

Dead records of Officers and Men found on the Battlefields of the Wilderness and Spottsylvania Court House Va — furnished by Quartermaster General U.S.A. on file in this Office. List of Casualties 4 Brig 1 Div 2 Corps from May 5 to July 16, 1864, shows the soldier was killed May 14, 1864, signed by H. A. Miles Actg Lieut. Div Comdr. J.W.

DEGREE OF DISABILITY

BY WHOM CERTIFIED.
Bvt Maj Genl M. C. Meigs

DATE OF DISCHARGE, DEATH, &c.
May 14" 1864

PLACE OF DISCHARGE, DEATH, &c.
Battlefield of the Wilderness or Spottsylvania Court House Va.

Chas E Forbes
Clerk.

Samuel's death Casualty Sheet

ARMY OF THE POTOMAC.

Certificate of Death.

I Certify, That Samuel Gonzallez [?] Captain Capt. Geo. A. Baird Company C of the 118th Regiment of Vols. 1st Brigade, 1st Division 2nd Corps, born in Overton Co. State of Tenn., aged 23 years; was enlisted by Geo. A. Lairlamb on the 8th day of August 1862, to serve for 3 years; died on the day of _____ 186_.

[Here state fully the Cause of Death.]

Private Samuel Gonzalino was killed at Spottsylvania Heights, Va., May 16th while in line of his duty.

Deceased Private Samuel Gonzalino was paid by Paymaster Maj. Oakley to include the 29th day of Feb. 186_, and has pay due from that time to date of death, May 16th 186_, being 2 months 16 days, at $13 4/7 per month, $34.50. The following amount of U.S. Bounty has been paid to him: 25 Dolls. There is due him 12 12/100 Dollars retained U.S. Bounty. There is due him _____ __/100 Dollars retained pay.

Samuel's Army Death Certificate

Samuel's headstone in the Fredericksburg National Cemetery[5]

Along with Samuel, H Company lost John Carlton. Thirteen others in the company were wounded; Corporal Robert Blackburn, Privates Uriah K. Brown, Robert Cassidy, John G. Deihl, Robert J. Kelly, George A. Wilson, Christian Stuck, William McKinney, William J. Lucas, George W. Freed, Robert Custard, William H. Klose, and John W. Moore.

The 148th regiment between the fighting at Po River and Spotsylvania lost a total of 33 men with 235 wounded and 33 missing; *"The greatest loss of any infantry regiment at Spotsylvania."*[2]

After the fierce battle subsided the 51st pulled back along with the 148th to another defensive position. The 51st lost 8 men, 75 wounded – 10 mortally, 33 captured, and 3 deserted. John's Company lost one man, Private Samuel Moore with Private Augustus Rolley being wounded.

Taylor and the 13th Cavalry, although at the battle, were held in reserve during the fighting. Although not in the main fight they did have a small skirmish here and there as they encountered Confederate picket lines.

During the 13 days of fighting at the Battle of Spotsylvania the Union lost 2,725 men with 13,416 wounded and 2,258 captured or missing. The Confederacy lost 1,515 men with 5,414 wounded and 5,758 captured or missing. All that death and carnage for a battle that was determined to have no victor.

It's not known how long it took John and Taylor to learn of their brother's death. The 13th Cavalry along with the 51st and 148th Infantry regiments would all fight at Cold Harbor in a few weeks and John and Taylor could have found out about it then because their Corps were fighting next to each other. Information took time to pass in the 1860's and with the confusion of war it probably took longer for the Army to inform Samuel's parents. From my research it appears that families usually found out about a loved one's death first by the wounded men returning home from the war, and later officially by the Army. In any case Samuel's parents eventually were officially notified of his death and received $111.47 due him; which was 2 months and 16 days of back pay, the remainder of his bounty, and the remainder of his clothing allowance.

Without Samuel the 148th went on to fight many more battles. And when the war ended *"It stands number thirty in the list of forty-five regiments that lost 200 and upward killed in battle, with the record of 210 men killed out of a total enrollment of 1339. It stands (notwithstanding the fact that it went out a year later then many of the regiments contained therein) number fourteen in the splendid "sifted" list of twenty three regiments which gave fifteen per cent and upwards of their blood for the flag."*[2]

As the fighting at the "Bloody Angle" subsided John's regiment held its position, and the Confederates did the same. This stalemate went on until the IX Corps pulled back on the 21st of May and headed for the Confederate capital of Richmond, Virginia. As the two remaining brothers headed south so did the Confederates. And as the two armies maneuvered their way to Richmond they played a tactical game of cat and mouse trying to catch each other in the open and off guard.

Taylor's regiment made a wide sweep to the left of Spotsylvania heading south to Richmond. As Taylor and the Cavalry scouted a path around the Confederate pickets John and the rest of IX Corps followed. As the IX Corps converged between the North and South Anna Rivers, Taylor's regiment was ordered to give up their horses and were converted to infantryman, or as they say "dismounted cavalrymen." The reason for giving up their horses wasn't that the Army needed more ground soldiers, it was that there was an extreme shortage of horses at the time. The 13th were giving up their horses to a veteran Cavalry regiment who was deemed better qualified to have them.

Taylor's 13th Cavalry crossed the Pamunkey River on the 27th of May and John's 51st the following day.

Taylor's Cavalry regiment was now moving ahead scouting toward Mechanicsville, Virginia in an attempt to secure a path for his advancing brother John and the IX Corps. At the same time the Confederate Cavalry was scouting north to try and figure out when and where the IX Corps would cross the Pamunkey River. The two opposing Cavalry forces met at Haw's Shop, Virginia on the 28th of May and engaged in one of the fiercest Calvary engagements of the war, although many of the men on both sides - like the 13th Cavalry, were dismounted. The engagement included the famous Union General George A. Custer, who was leading his Brigade of Michigan "Wolverines."

The battle was officially a draw even though the Confederates withdrew because both sides came away with positives. The Confederates had determined where the Union force was located, and had held them up fighting for several hours. And the Union force maintained its presence and advanced on the road to Richmond. For the 13th Cavalry the loss was 6 men with 28 wounded. Taylor's Company lost Sergeant James Floyd who was mortally wounded. Figures vary for the Union and Confederacy on casualties but a consensus seems to be about a combined total of 800 men killed, wounded and missing.

John and Taylor eventually converged with each other just north of Richmond. Taylor's 13th Calvary arrived just outside of Richmond at Cold Harbor on the 31st of May. Although the Calvary was actively engaged in fighting on the 1st of June, Taylor's regiment was held in reserve. And John and the 51st arrived at Cold Harbor on the 1st of June. In transit from Spotsylvania the 51st skirmished with the enemy several times losing 3 men with 1 wounded, 10 captured and 1 deserter. John's Company lost Private Charles Prescott.

The 51st were placed north of the city of Cold Harbor and engaged the enemy on the 1st and 2nd in light skirmishes. Then at daylight on the 3rd they were ordered, along with a massive Union force, to attack the heavily fortified Confederate defensive position. As John and the 51st charged they crossed an open field under heavy fire before engaging the enemy. Reaching the Confederate position they drove them from their first line of defense. The regiment fought until dark when they were relieved and fell back to a safe position.

In what was later deemed a suicide attack the Union force sustained heavy losses. The 51st lost its Commanding Officer, Lieutenant Colonel Edwin Schall along with 10 others. Fifty-two more were wounded and of those 8 mortally.

John's Company lost Private Emil Held with Private Charles Prescott mortally wounded and Privates Lewis Cartinwells and Reuben Hinet wounded.

The death of Colonel Schall is described by Major Bolton; *"During the charge and at 5 ½ A.M. Lt. Col. Schall was shot dead at my side, and the command of the regiment fell on me. Schall's body laid on the field until after dark, as it would have been certain death to have attempted to recover it in daylight………..but after dark his body, as well as the rest of the killed, were recovered. Schall was universally loved by the whole regiment, and his loss was severely felt."*[12]

The Battle of Cold Harbor was considered a Confederate victory as they held their fortification. The cost to the Union Army in attacking such a fortified position was astounding - losing 1,844 men with 9,077 wounded and 1,816 missing or captured. The Confederates lost 788 men with 3,376 wounded and 1,123 missing or captured.

After the Battle of Cold Harbor, Taylor's regiment held up at New Castle Ferry, Virginia. John and his regiment, now commanded by Lieutenant Colonel William J. Bolton stayed at their fortification near Cold Harbor until the 13th of June when they headed south and crossed the Chickahominy and James Rivers.

On the 5th of June Taylor and the 13th Cavalry, with their horses returned, prepared to go out on a raid with a large union Cavalry force. The mission was twofold; first to draw the Confederate Calvary away from the Union Army moving south to Richmond and second to destroy parts of the Virginia Central Railroad. *"In preparation for another raid, three days rations of hardtack were issued to the men. In addition, nine tablespoons each of coffee and sugar were handed out, as well as two days of forage for the horses, which was strapped to the pommels of the saddles. One hundred rounds of ammunition were issued per man; forty to be carried and sixty more transported in the wagons."*[10]

The Calvary force headed out traveling northwest and by the 8th of June they camped near the Polecat Station on the Richmond and Potomac Railroad. On the 9th the force camped at Young's Mill, Virginia. And on the 10th they were just outside of Travilian Station where they camped at Clayton's Store, Virginia. All that traveling in enemy territory and they had not been detected. On the morning of the 11th the Union Calvary headed into Travilian Station to secure the railroad.

Meanwhile the Confederate Calvary had been out looking for the Union Calvary and were just on the other side of Travilian Station. As they both rode in to the station on the 11th of June the largest and bloodiest Calvary engagement of the war was waged.

Taylor's regiment, along with most of the Union force, hit the Confederates head on and drove them from the station while General Custer's men hit them on their flank. After clearing out the Confederates, Taylor and the Union Calvary began to tear up the railroad tracks. The next day Taylor and the Union force once again attacked the Confederates but this time they were ready and repulsed them. With heavy casualties and running low on ammunition and supplies Taylor and the Union force withdrew from the battle. The cost to the Union was 95 men killed, 445 wounded, and 410 missing or captured. The Confederates lost a total of 813 men but the breakdown of killed, wounded, and missing is unknown. Taylor's Regiment lost 1 man with 2 wounded and 2 captured.

After the engagement, Taylor and the Union force started to make their way south toward Petersburg, Virginia. They were tasked with escorting a wagon train of supplies. As they provided a protective escort the 13th Cavalry lost 1 man with 2 captured and 1 deserter as they skirmished with the Confederates all the way to St. Mary's Church, Virginia.

As the Confederates shadowed the Union force and wagon train south, their plan was to engage them once they crossed the Chickahominy River at St. Mary's Church. As planned they met on the 24th of June as Taylor and the Union supply column had crossed the river. The Confederates had the advantage of surprise and they outnumbered the Union 5 brigades to 2. But Taylor and his comrades put up a fight and although outnumbered, they held their ground. Each side lost about 300 men each and the Union continued south as the Confederates pulled back to Petersburg. Taylor and the 13th Cavalry were covering the Union's flank and was heavily involved in the fighting, losing 2 men with 14 wounded and 28 missing.

Continuing south John and the 51st crossed the James River on the 15th of June as they marched with the rest of the Union Army toward Petersburg.

Bridge over the James River that John and the 51st crossed on the 15th of June[16]

John and the 51st arrived at Petersburg and engaged the Confederates on the 17th of June. Advancing on a railroad line that was cut into a hillside 25 feet deep, the regiment ran into heavy fighting. The loss was 8 men killed with 20 wounded - 4 mortally and 1 deserter. John's Company lost Private Bartley McLarney. That evening the regiment along with the rest of the Union force dug in. The following day they once again engaged the enemy. This time the 51st lost 3 men with 26 wounded – 2 mortally. John's Company lost Private William Young and Private George Rodgers was wounded.

The 51st remained on the front lines skirmishing with the Confederates until the 18th of July when they were relieved and went into reserves. During their time on the front lines they lost 6 more men with 7 more wounded.

And so the long siege of Petersburg began.

After finishing their wagon train escort duty Taylor and the 13th Cavalry patrolled east of Richmond and Petersburg destroying or taking all the crops, cattle, and anything else they came across. Their job was to make life as tough as possible for the Confederate Army and their sympathizers. By the 16th of July they were guarding the Petersburg, Weldon & Danville Railroad and protecting the main Union Army's flank.

John and the 51st Infantry were still maintaining their siege position at Petersburg. They spent their days going out on picket duty and exchanging artillery fire with the Confederates who were situated in a well-built fortification. As the stalemate over Petersburg dragged on, a plan was devised by the Union Army to tunnel under the Confederate fortress and blow it up. Well not actually the whole thing, just a portion of the protective wall of one side. With the wall gone, the Union Army could gain access to the fortress through the opening.

On the 30th of July the tunnel full of explosives was detonated, followed by a barrage of over 350 artillery pieces. As planned, the explosion caused a huge gap in the Confederate fortification along with an enormous crater. John and the 51st were in the second wave of Union infantry to pour through the crater. *"At 1 P.M. the bottom sides, and nearly all parts of the crater were strewn with dead, dying, and wounded soldiers, causing pools of blood to be formed at the bottom of the cater."*[12]

Initially the Union attack went as planned and they penetrated into the fortification. But as the Confederates reorganized and counter attacked they drove the Union force back to their starting position. In the fighting the 51st lost 4 men with 20 wounded – 2 mortally and 3 captured. In John's Company Private Daniel Sheets was mortally wounded, Privates Abraham King and James Hall wounded, and Private Jacob Casher was captured.

One of the men in the 51st who was wounded was their Commanding Officer, Colonel Bolton. Ironically he sustained a bullet wound to the face in the same location of a wound he received at Antietam. Due to his inability to command he was relieved by Major Lane S. Hart.

After the unsuccessful attack on the fortress the 51st along with the rest of the Union force returned to their starting position and resumed their watchful eye over the fortification.

By the 13th of August Taylor and the 13th Cavalry had moved south of Petersburg and were still skirmishing on a daily basis. On the 14th they crossed the James River on maneuvers and ran into Confederate Calvary scouts at Deep Bottom, Virginia. In the skirmish the 13th Cavalry lost 1 man with 6 wounded and 5 missing. Of these casualties Taylor's M Company had 3 men mortally wounded - Privates John Moor, Joseph M. Stocker, and William Smith.

John and the 51st were ordered from their fortifications on the 19th of August to proceed to Globe Tavern, Virginia which was on the south side of the Confederate fortification of Petersburg. Taylor and the 13th Cavalry were in route to another assignment but were also diverted to Globe Tavern. During a rainy and stormy day on the 19th both John and Taylor engaged the Confederates at the Battle of Globe Tavern - also known as the 2nd Battle of the Weldon Railroad. This was a strategic Confederate railroad station helping to keep supplies flowing into Petersburg.

Globe Tavern

After several days of fighting, from the 19th to the 21st, the Confederates withdrew leaving parts of the railway in Union hands.

The Union lost 251 men with 1,148 wounded and 2,897 captured or missing. The Confederates lost 211 men with 990 wounded and 419 captured or missing.

It was a tough day for the 51st and they lost 4 men with 32 wounded – 2 mortally, and 29 captured. Out of those men John's Company lost Private Christian Sheets. Wounded were Lieutenant Curtin B. Stoneroad and Privates George Dulott, R.C. Hollabaugh, and Thomas Moser. Sergeants Louis Cartuyvel, J.J. Peters, and Private George Larrah were captured. To make matters worse the 51st's newly assigned Commanding Officer, Major Hart, was wounded three times. Unable to maintain command he was relieved by Captain Joseph K. Bolton, who was the previous commanding officers son. Captain Bolton led his men back to their entrenchments overlooking Petersburg.

Taylor and the 13th Cavalry lost 6 men with 22 wounded and 39 captured.

After the engagement Taylor and the 13th Cavalry headed south to destroy more railroad tracks leading to Petersburg. By the 22nd of August they were at Ream's Station, Virginia. Knowing how vital this location was to their dwindling supply lines the Confederates raced to protect it. On the 25th the two forces collided and the Confederates managed to push the Union force back from the station, although not before a good portion of the tracks were destroyed by the Union.

At Ream's Station the Union lost 140 men with 529 wounded and 2,073 captured. The Confederates lost a total of 814 men.

Taylor's 13th Cavalry lost 2 men with 4 captured and remained in the area of Ream's Station conducting picket duty.

As the siege of Petersburg dragged on, the huge Union Army needed to be kept fed and part of the food supply came from a herd of almost 3,000 head of cattle. They were kept under guard at Coggins Point, Virginia which is located north east of Petersburg. Since the Union Army had been destroying their rail supply lines, the Confederates were running low on food and faced starvation at Petersburg. So they devised a plan to capture the Union cattle.

On the 16th of September Companies B, C and D of the 13th Cavalry were helping 60 civilian cattlemen guard the cattle. Taylor and M Company were kept on picket duty near Ream's Station. The Confederate Cavalry, following their plan, attacked and made off with over 2,000 head of cattle. The 3 Companies of the 13th Cavalry were pretty beaten up in the affair losing 2 men with 8 wounded and 29 captured. The civilian cattlemen had 2 men killed, 1 wounded and 13 captured. It was a bad day for the 13th Cavalry in casualties and lost cattle.

As John and the 51st held their position at Petersburg they routinely engaged in skirmishes and exchanged artillery fire with the Confederates inside the besieged city. And on the 27th of October they participated in a reconnaissance mission to try and find a weak spot in the Confederate defenses. After engaging with the enemy near the Clements House they sustained 17 wounded – 1 mortally.

For the majority of November John and the 51st were assigned to the defensive position in front of Petersburg known as Fort Sampson. Here on the 8th of November John and the regiment cast their votes for the Presidential Election between the incumbent, Republican Abraham Lincoln, and the challenger, Democrat George McClellan. The 51st counted 253 votes for Lincoln and 145 for McClellan. Even though McClellan was a Union General and at one point in charge of the Union Army I'm sure John voted Republican and for Lincoln, who won the election. I'm not sure how Taylor voted, but political affiliation usually runs in a family so I assume he was also a Republican.

In late November the 51st moved to Fort Morton which was located just in front of the "crater." At both locations they stood picket duty and exchanged artillery barrages with the Confederates.

After the setback for the 13th Cavalry at Coggins Point they regrouped and continued on picket duty south of Petersburg. On the 1st of December they were detailed with a Union force to head even further south to determine if the Confederates were moving troops out of Petersburg and to destroy the southern supply depot at Stony Creek Station, Virginia. Arriving that day the Union force met little resistance and burned the station and surrounding buildings to the ground. They marched back to their encampment near Lees Mill, Virginia with as much captured supplies as they could carry, and destroyed everything in their path.

Fort Morton, pictured to the left of the "crater" at Petersburg

By the 7th of December Taylor and the 13th Cavalry were once again on the move, this time to Hatcher's Run, Virginia which is just south west of Petersburg. After encountering the enemy, but not breaking through its defenses, the regiment moved back to camp. The 13th Cavalry sustained 7 wounded men in the engagement.

The year ended on a positive note for Taylor as he received $60.00, the second installment on his enlistment bounty.

1865

The New Year began with John and Taylor within 5 miles of each other at Petersburg, Virginia. Taylor and the 13th Cavalry were encamped where they had been for the past few months, about 5 miles south of Petersburg. They remained there conducting picket duty until February.

John and the 51st were still encamped at Fort Morton just in front of the "crater" which was created from the explosion back on the 30th of July.

As the siege dragged on more and more Confederate deserters were leaving besieged Petersburg and crossing over into the Union lines. Hungry and tired of the war they figured life would be easier in a prisoner of war camp. Although a crime, desertion was common on both sides and you probably noticed that in just about every major battle that has been mentioned in this book that men have deserted. Whatever their reason for leaving, they either surrendered to the opposite side or tried to get past their own lines to make it back home. But surrendering was much easier and safer. If you were caught by your own side, desertion was punishable with death. And men on both sides were executed in front of their regiment for the crime.

After 2nd Lieutenant Curtin B. Stoneroad was wounded on the 19th of August at Globe Tavern, John applied for an officer's commission to fill his vacancy. On the 14th of January his request was approved and John was promoted to 2nd Lieutenant and remained in G Company. He was now making $105.50 a month as an officer, a big increase from his starting salary of $13.00 a month as a private. It was also a huge accomplishment. Not many men entered the Army as a private and promoted to the rank of a commissioned officer. The position of an officer usually required an educated man, and because of this I feel John penned his own letters which you will see on the following pages.

John didn't remain a 2nd Lieutenant for long and was promoted to 1st Lieutenant while still opposite the "crater" on the 13th of February. The promotion brought on more responsibility but his pay remained the same - $105.50 a month. To make the day even more eventful G Company had an artillery shell explode on one of their barracks knocking off a bunch of logs and filling it with dirt. Luckily no one was injured.

Camp 51st Regt. Pa. Vet. Vols.
January 14th 1865

Capt Jno. C. Youngman
A. A. G.

Capt.

In Compliance with Circular of December 7th 1864 from Hd Qrs. 9th A. C. I respectfully make Application for a discharge to enable me to recieve promotion. I certify that I have this day recieved and accepted a Commission as 2nd Lieut of Co. "G" issued by the Gov. of Pa on the 3rd day of January 1865 to fill vacancy caused by the discharge of 2nd Lieut Curtin P. Seneca on account of disability on the 28th day of Dec. 1864. I further certify that I entered upon the duties of 2nd Lieut of Co. "G" on the 14th day January 1865.

The following is a brief history of past Services rendered. I entered the Service at Snow-Shoe, Centre Co. Pa under Capt A. B. Snyder on the 16th day of Sept. 1861. and was mustered into the U.S. Service on the 20th day of 1861 by Capt. R. I. Dodge at Harrisburg Pa. for the period of three (3) years. Was promoted Corporal the 1st day of Oct. 1862 and served as such un the 20th day of March 1863 when I was promoted First Sergt of Co. "G." I was discharged the Service on the 31st day of Dec 1863 by virtue of Re-enlistment. Re-enlisted Jan 1st 1864 by Lieut Wm R. Foster and was mustered into the U.S. Service on the 1st day of Jan. 1864 by Lieut Bartlett, for three years. I have participated in the following named engagements, Roanoke Island, Newbern, Camden, 2nd Bull Run, Chantilly, South Mountain, Antietam, Fredericksburg, the Campaign of Mississippi and East Tennessee, and the engagements of the present Campaign since May 4th 1864.

I am Capt most Respectfully
your Obedient Servt
John Grinsalles
1st Sergt Co "G" 57th Regt P.V.

John's letter requesting promotion to 2nd Lieutenant

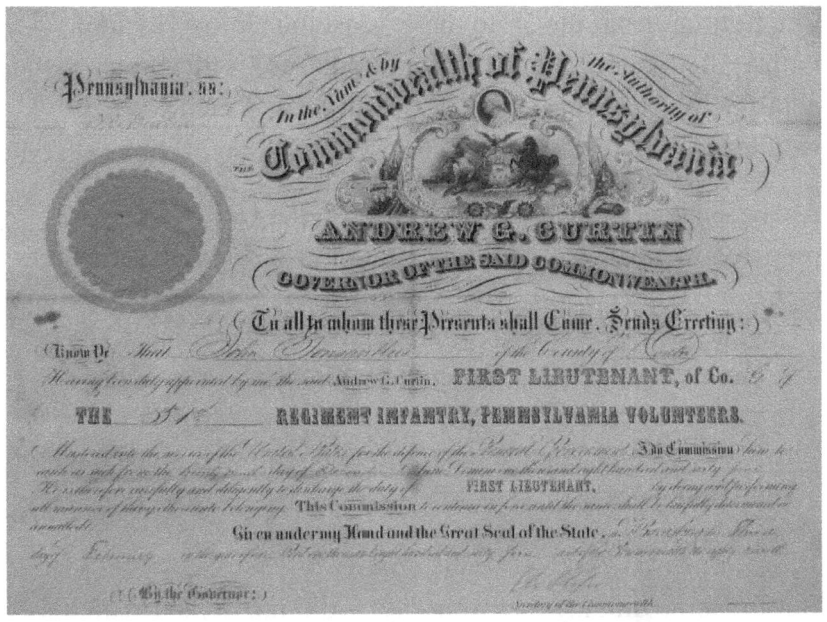

John's promotion certificate to 1st Lieutenant

Taylor and the 13th Cavalry were mounted up and moving on the 5th of February and headed south once again to cut off Confederate supply lines into Petersburg. By afternoon they had arrived at Hatcher's Run, Virginia and with a larger Union force engaged the Confederates. During the fighting on the 6th Sergeant Daniel Caldwell of H Company was part of a mounted charge into an enemy position. Sergeant Caldwell dashed into the center of the 33rd North Carolina Infantry's battle line and captured their colors along with 5 prisoners. He was subsequently awarded the Medal of Honor and promoted to 2nd Lieutenant for his actions that day.

The fighting from the 5th to the 7th cost the Union 171 men with 1,181 wounded and 187 captured. The Confederates lost a combined 1,161 men. The 13th Cavalry lost 4 men with 10 wounded.

As the siege at Petersburg continued on the Union Army prepared to advance on North Carolina in a separate campaign. General Ulysses Grant, who was in charge of the entire Union Army, needed a Cavalry regiment to assist the Union force he was deploying there. He directed his Calvary commander to select a top of the line Cavalry regiment and Taylor's 13th Cavalry was selected. They had come a long way since having to give their horses up 9 months ago and had proven they were a veteran Calvary regiment.

But for some unknown reason Taylor did not deploy with his regiment. Instead he was reassigned on detached duty to the Cavalry's 2nd Brigade Headquarters which stayed at the siege of Petersburg.

In late February as Taylor settled in with his new command his comrades in M Company along with the rest of the 13th Cavalry deployed to North Carolina.

On the 18th of March while the 51st was still at Fort Morton in front of the "crater" John requested leave to go home. His mother Ruth was sick with Typhoid Fever and he feared she would not survive it. The request was apparently denied because his Company Muster Roll Card indicates he was present at his unit for all of March. Also, the Union Army was undertaking a massive troop shift during this time period and the 51st was one of the only regiments held in place while the others shifted around Petersburg.

Camp 51st Regt, Penn'a, Vet. Vols
March 18th 1865

Capt John C. Youngman
A. A. Genl. 9th A.C.

Capt
I would most respectfully make application for leave of absence for fifteen (15) days, to visit my home in Centre County, Penn'a, for the following reasons.
I have received intelligence of the serious illness of my Mother, who is suffering with the Typhoid fever. She is aged, and cannot possibly live through that dangerous disease. I desire to see her very much, therefore I hope the above will meet with your approval.
I am, Capt
Very respectfully
Your Obt. Servt
John Gansallus
1st Lieutent. G. 51st P.V.

John's request for leave to visit his sick mother

It's unclear if Taylor requested or was granted leave to go home because his Company Muster Roll Cards are missing from the period he was attached to Brigade Headquarters. Surely if John knew that their mother was sick Taylor who was fighting nearby would have also known. In any case John and

Taylor's mother survived the Typhoid Fever and went on to live until 1892.

As Taylor and John stood vigil over Petersburg in March the Confederates were devising a plan to try and break out of the siege. As an increasing number of Confederate deserters made their way over into the Union lines the Confederates planned to use this to their advantage. The plan was to send a huge force of armed men into the Union lines on the pretense of surrendering, but with the motive of attacking.

On the morning of the 25th of March the Confederate plan was unleashed on the unsuspecting Union Army. Coming across the lines north of John and Taylor, at the Union fortification known as Fort Stedman, thousands of armed Confederates walked into the Union lines pretending to surrender. Once behind the Union lines they attacked. After they made huge gains into the Union interior they were eventually repulsed and captured by night fall. The loss to the Union was 72 men with 450 wounded and 522 captured or missing. The Confederates lost 600 men with 2,400 wounded and 1,000 captured or missing.

On the 1st of April, Taylor and the 2nd Brigade were sweeping wide of Petersburg to the south and confronted the Confederates at the Battle of Five Forks. The maneuver was to secure the South Side Railroad and it was an overwhelming Union victory. While taking control of the railroad the Union force inflicted over 830 Confederate casualties and captured 2,950 men.

Captured Confederates at the Battle of Five Forks[6]

Meanwhile back in Petersburg the failed sneak attack on the 25th of March did not thwart the Confederates ambition to break out of the city and they attacked for the next couple of days. On the 2nd of April John, and the rest of the Union force made an attack on the city. The 51st lost 1 man with two wounded. The following day Petersburg had fallen and the Confederates pulled way as the Union force moved in. Finally after almost 10 months, John and the 51st were vacating their fortifications and moving through Petersburg. The siege had cost the Union Army around 42,000 casualties and the Confederates 28,000.

John states in an interview[9] that he was slightly wounded twice while at the siege of Petersburg. I was unable to ascertain any information surrounding the events of these wounds and there is no mention of them in his service record. Perhaps they were superficial wounds and he mended them on his own without reporting them, which was a common practice.

By the 5th of April the 51st was near Sutherland, Virginia which is about 10 miles west of Petersburg. And by the following day they had made camp on a Confederate colonel's plantation at Wilson's Station, Virginia. On the 9th they made it to Blacks and Whites, Virginia to guard the South Side Railroad depot there, unchallenged by the Confederates. The protected access to the railroad was made possible by Taylor and his Union force back on the 1st when they secured Five Forks.

Now guarding the railroad at Blacks and Whites John watched as daily trains carried Union troops headed to the front lines. And when they returned they carried Confederate prisoners by the thousands back to the rear.

It seemed the war was coming to an end. I'm sure John and Taylor could feel the changing tide as they chased the Confederates. And then on the 14th of April came the news that President Abraham Lincoln was assassinated by a Confederate sympathizer. Days later the war was over.

On the 20th of April John and the 51st were ordered to pack up and proceed to Washington, DC. By the 22nd they were at City Point, Virginia and boarded the *S.S. Cossack*. On the 24th they had arrived in Washington, DC. and encamped on the Fowle Farm near Fairfax, Virginia.

Taylor was released from Brigade Headquarters and sent back to the 13th Cavalry, rejoining them on the 30th of April in Fayetteville, North Carolina. Here they were tasked with providing law enforcement.

John and the 51st in Fairfax were also tasked with providing law enforcement and guarding Confederate prisoners. On the 23rd of May they participated in the Grand Review of the troops in Washington, DC. This huge parade consisted of over 100,000 soldiers. It was such a huge event that John and the 51st had to leave their camp a day before the parade to get into position. Early in the morning on the 23rd they were formed up in the procession and proceeded to march down the streets of Washington. As they marched through the city they were cheered by the crowds lining their path. The climax was passing the review stand of newly installed President Andrew Johnson.

The Grand Review of the Army on the 23rd of May 1865 in Washington, DC. [17]

While John marched through Washington, Taylor was protecting North Carolina. On the 28th of June Taylor and the 13th Cavalry were moved to Raleigh, North Carolina and the Cavalry Corps was dissolved. On the 14th of July while still in Raleigh he was mustered-out of the service with most of his regiment. When mustered-out he was given his final pay and bounty and was allowed to take home his revolver, sabre, and complete belt. The following day Taylor and his regiment boarded a train at City Point, Virginia which took them to Philadelphia, Pennsylvania were they were officially discharged. I'm sure Taylor headed straight home from there, excited to get back and be with his family.

When you look at Taylor's Muster-Out Card on the following page you'll find that it reveals some really interesting information about his revolver and sabre which I previously mentioned. But what caught my attention was that it states his correct age of 18 years. We know that back in March of 1864 he lied about his age on his enlistment contract, stating he was 19 years old. It seems his real age had caught up to him.

John was mustered-out of the service on the 27th of July in Alexandria, Virginia. Like Taylor he was allowed to keep his gun and equipment at a cost of $6 per item. And on the 29th he and the regiment boarded trains to Harrisburg, Pennsylvania arriving there the following day. As they marched through the decorated city to their old encampment at Camp Curtin they were given a hero's welcome. From there the different companies and men went their separate ways.

I'm sure John also headed straight for home to see his family. There he should have found Taylor who had arrived a few days earlier.

| G | 13 Cav. | Pa. |

Taylor Gonsallas

Prt., Co. M.C., 13 Reg't Pennsylvania Cav.

Age 18 years.

Appears on **Co. Muster-out Roll,** dated
Raleigh, N.C. July 14, 1865.
Muster-out to date July 14, 1865.
Last paid to Dec. 31, 1864.

Clothing account:
Last settled Mch. 8, 1864; drawn since $ 69 53/100
Due soldier $ .... 100/100; due U. S. $ 100/100
Am't for cloth'g in kind or money adv'd $ 100/100

Due U. S. for arms, equipments, &c., $ 100/100
Bounty paid $ 100 00/100; due $ 200 00/100
Valuation of horse, $ 100/100
Valuation of horse equipments, $ 100/100
Remarks: Takes home 1 Rem. Revolver, Sabre & Belt complete.

Book mark:

(861) Armstrong
Copyist.

Taylor's Muster out Card

Post War

When the war ended John and Taylor like most every other soldier returned to society, found employment, and got on with their lives.

John had spent over 4 years away from home fighting, almost the entire duration of the Civil War. After returning home to Snow Shoe, Pennsylvania he worked as a farmer and lumberman on his father's farm. After a few months he decided to head west. His sweetheart, Pamelia Lucas had relocated with her parents from Centre County, Pennsylvania to West Union, Iowa during the war and John moved there to marry her. After getting married on the 11th of October 1865 in West Union John and Pamelia settled down there. But the two decided that Iowa wasn't meant for them and after a year relocated back to Snow Shoe.

Settled back in Pennsylvania they had 7 children; Samuel, Margaret, Ida, Nora, Harry, Ruth, and Clara. I can only speculate that their first child, Samuel, was named in memory of John's brother who was lost at Spotsylvania.

John spent the rest of his life in Snow Shoe and was very active in the community. He served 4 years as a Township Supervisor and 3 terms as the Tax Collector. He was also a member of the Independent Order of Odd Fellows - I.O.O.F, The Knights of Pythias, and the American Mechanics.

The government passed the Dependent and Disability Pension Act in June of 1890 and the following year John applied for, and was granted, a Civil War pension for his war time service.

John and his first son Samuel share a headstone in Askey Cemetery

Living a full life and reaching the age of 80 years John passed away on the 7th of May 1918. A well-known man throughout central Pennsylvania an article in the Indiana Evening Gazette many years after his death fittingly *"ranked (him) with John*

Askey as the greatest hunter in Centre County, and was a terror to the wolves and panthers of the region."[14]

Adjutant General's Office,
Washington, D. C.
Oct 1st, 1866.

Sir:

I have the honor to acknowledge the receipt of your letter of the _____ day of _____, 186_, requesting a "Statement of Service" of _____. The following information has been obtained from the files of this Office, and is respectfully furnished in reply to your inquiry:

It appears from the Rolls on file in this Office, that Samuel Gunsaulles was enrolled on the _____ day of Aug, 1862, at Bellefonte Pa, in Co. H, 145th Regiment of Pa Volunteers, to serve 3 years, or during the war, and mustered into service as a Pvt, on the 16th day of Aug, 1862 at Harrisburg Pa in Co. H, 148 Regiment of Pa Volunteers, to serve 3 years, or during the war. On the Muster Roll of Co. H of that Regiment for the months of May & June, 1864, he is reported "Killed May 10, 1864."

The name Saml. Gunsatius is not borne _____

I am, sir, very respectfully,
Your obedient servant,

_____
Assistant Adjutant General.

To D&D.R.R.,
AGO,

Post war letter dated 1866 concerning Samuel's death

Samuel served 1 year and 9 months of war time service and witnessed some of the fiercest battles fought on American soil. Although losing his life in the war, he posthumously helped support his parents by way of a Civil War death pension that they applied for in 1879.

Taylor served 1 year and 4 months of war time service and was the youngest of the three brothers to enlist. He also remained in Snow Shoe and worked as a farmer and in the coal industry. He married Elexia Culver in 1869 and they had three children; Meese, Ottis, and Franklin.

Taylor's marriage to Elexia has a coincidental connection to his fallen brother Samuel. Elexia's father served with Samuel in the 148th Infantry, but in a different company. Lewis Culver was 43 years old when he and Samuel served together, and because of his age he could have acted as a father figure or mentor to Samuel who was only 21. They did join the regiment at the same time and were both from Snow Shoe, so they would have had a lot in common. I could not find any documentation that Taylor and Elexia met as a result of Samuel and Lewis knowing each other, but it is an interesting connection.

Taylor was granted a Civil War pension in 1890 and this helped offset his income. But still having to work he moved to Westmoreland County, Pennsylvania in 1900 and was working for the Pittsburg Coal Company along with his son Ottis. His other two sons were also working as coal miners but in Cambria County, Pennsylvania.

On the 10th of June 1901 Taylor was working as a loader and Ottis as a roadman in the #1 shaft of the Port Royal Mines situated along the Youghiogheny River. There was a horrific explosion and Taylor and several other men were killed. Wanting to get in and save his father Ottis volunteered to enter the mine and look for survivors. Subsequent explosions rocked the mine and Ottis was also lost. In total 19 miners were killed that day. Taylor was 54 years old and Ottis 28 years old. After Taylor's death his wife Elexia applied for a widow's Civil War pension to help support her.

Taylor is buried with Elexia and Ottis at the Askey Cemetery in Snow Shoe where they are surrounded by family. Ottis's grave is marked but Taylor's and Elexia's are not.

My wife and I have been to Askey Cemetery on several occasions conducting genealogy research. Many of the Gunsallus' and their extended family are buried there. It is a very old and peaceful cemetery located just out of town and a few miles from Gunsallus Road. As I walk the rows of the cemetery I am always amazed at the number of men who fought in the Civil War from this small community. The patriotism and pride of these families is evident in the way they recognized their family members' Civil War service by listing their company and regiment on their headstones.

Speaking of my wife, her great-great-grandfather Sam Houston Walker also fought in the Civil War - but for the Confederacy. He served from 1862 to 1865 and was attached to a regiment from the state of Missouri. He fought in numerous battles in

Arkansas and Louisiana and settled in Texas after surviving the war. Fortunately he was never in an engagement with the Gunsallus brothers.

So ends the Civil War story of John, Samuel, and Taylor. I think their war service exemplifies what most men endured on both sides of the fighting during the Civil War. They were in battles won and lost, some unharmed and some killed.

Their stories are those of the men of their time. And like the men of their time they are gone but should never be forgotten.

Resources

1. History of Pennsylvania Volunteers, 1861-5
Prepared in compliance with acts of the legislature
By Samuel P. Bates, Author: Bates, Samuel P. (Samuel Penniman),
827-1902

2. The Story of Our Regiment, A History of The 148th Pennsylvania Volunteers.
By the Comrades; Edited by Adjt. J. W. Muffly; published by The Kenyon Printing and Mfg. Company, Des Moines, Iowa. 1904

3. Pennsylvania State Archives, Harrisburg

4. The Pennsylvania Civil War Project/Pennsylvanians in the Civil War
By Steve Maczuga

5. www.findagrave.com

6. Library of Congress uncredited work

7. The Raftsman's Journal of Clearfield County, dated 26 March 1862.
By S.J. Row

8. Pennsylvania Historical and Museum Commission

9. Commemorative Biographical Record of Central Pennsylvania: Including the Counties of Centre, Clearfield, Jefferson and Clarion: Containing Biographical Sketches of Prominent and Representative Citizens, Etc.
By J.H. Beers - 1898 Chicago

10. One Good Regiment – The 13th Pennsylvania Calvary in the Civil War, 1861 – 1865
By Harold Hand, JR.

11. Descendants of Samuel Gonsalus
By Wayne E. Andrews

12. The Civil War Journal of Colonel William J. Bolton
Edited by Richard A. Sauers

13. History of the 51st Regiment of Pennsylvania Volunteers
By Thomas Parker

14. Indiana Evening Gazette, dated 11 May 1950
By J.R. Williams

15. The Union County Star and Lewisburg Chronicle

16. Alexander Gardner (1821 – 1882), Photographer
Library of Congress

17. Mathew B. Brady (1823 – 1896), Photographer
Library of Congress

18. Andrew J. Russell, Photographer
Library of Congress
19. G. O. Brown, Photographer
Library of Congress

20. Timothy H. O'Sullivan (1840 – 1882), Photographer
Library of Congress

About the Author

Ed Semler retired from the United States Coast Guard in December of 2007 with over 25 years of military service in both the United States Army and United States Coast Guard. In the United States Army he was an enlisted man and was honorably discharged as a specialist four (E-4). While in the United States Coast Guard he was enlisted, obtaining the rank of master chief petty officer (E-9), was commissioned as an officer, and retired as a lieutenant (O-3E).

After his military career Ed dabbled in teaching at a Vocational Technical School and was a self-employed plumber for several years. As a past time he enjoys writing.

His other publications are "Around The World," which details his 25 years of service as an officer and enlisted man in the U.S. Army and U.S. Coast Guard along with "U.S. Coast Guard Cutter Sherman (WHEC-720) Circumnavigation Deployment 2001," which details the *Sherman's* historic circumnavigation of the globe and deployment to the Persian Gulf in 2001.

Fully retired he resides in Schulenburg, Texas with his wife Jana, a retired Air Force senior master sergeant. Please feel free to contact him at semlercreek@yahoo.com